AF394711

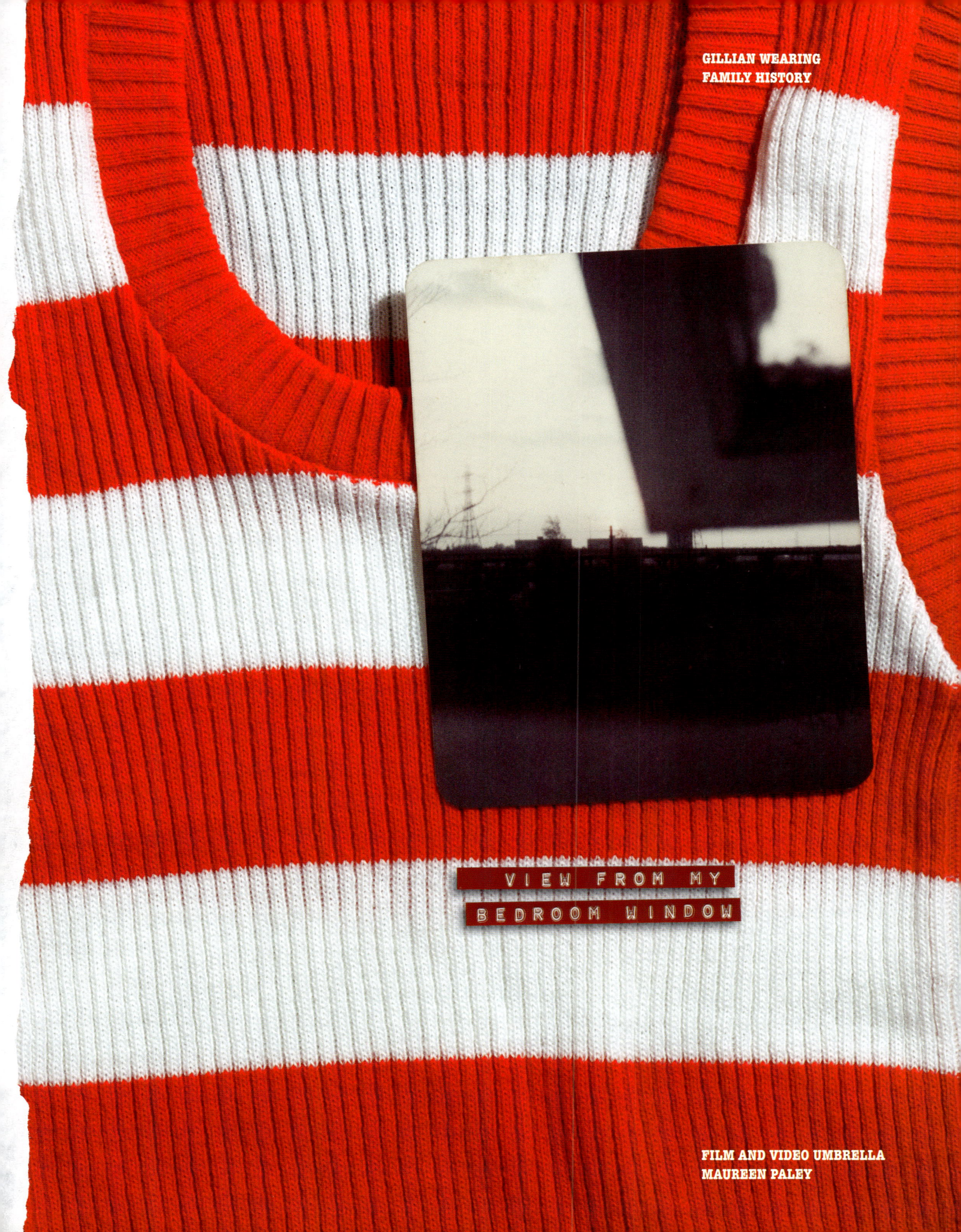

GILLIAN WEARING
FAMILY HISTORY

VIEW FROM MY
BEDROOM WINDOW

FILM AND VIDEO UMBRELLA
MAUREEN PALEY

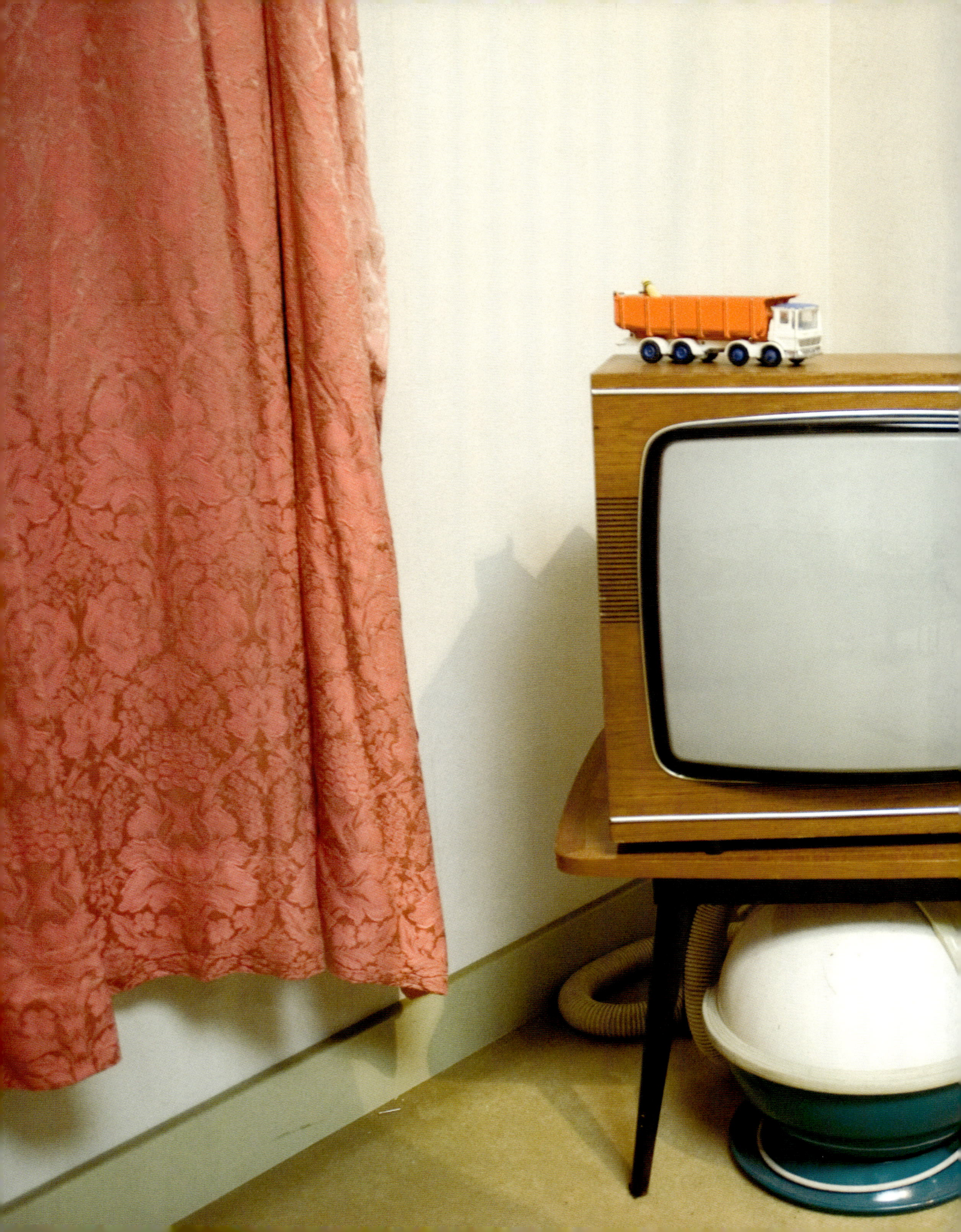

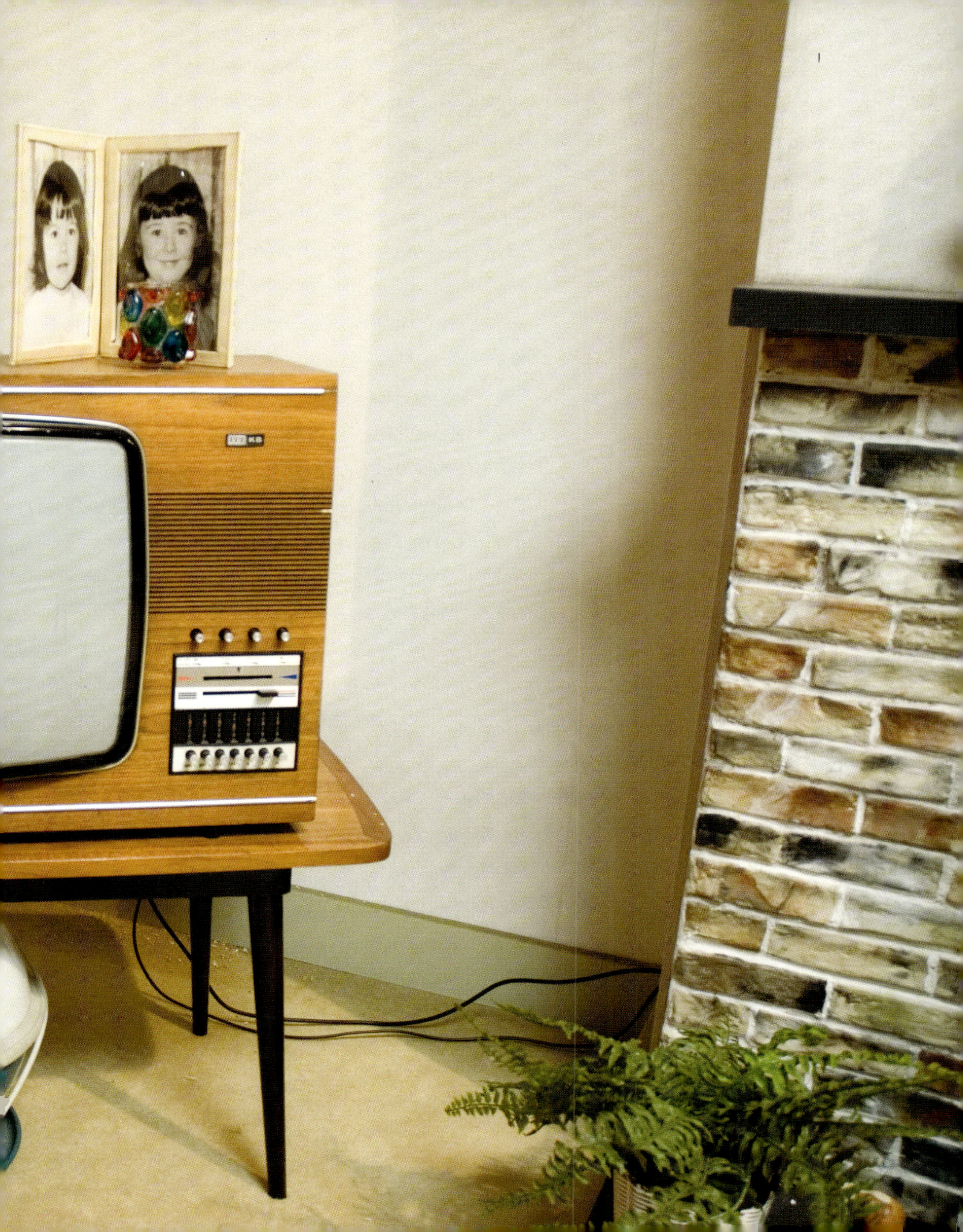

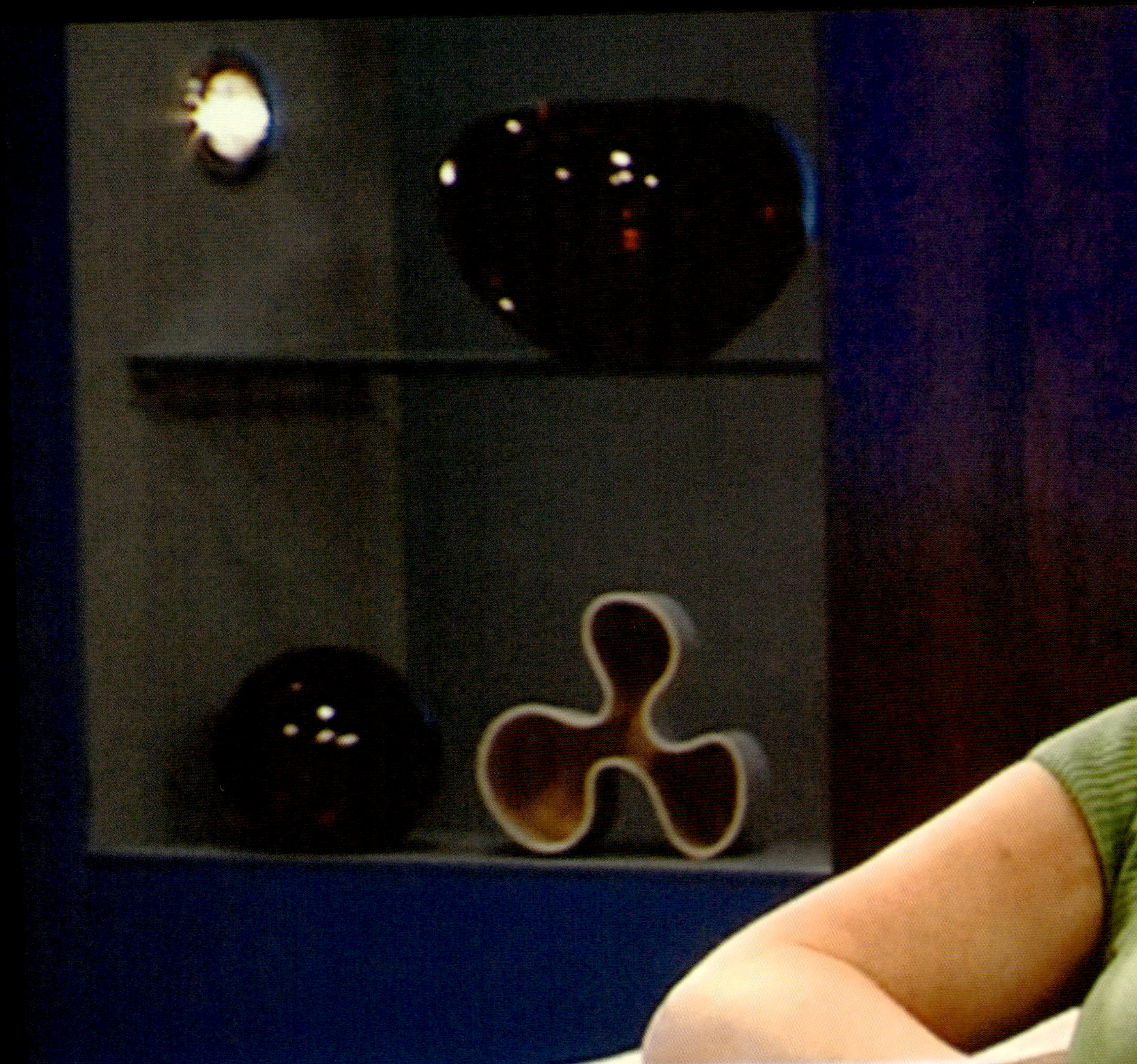
HEATHER WILKINS

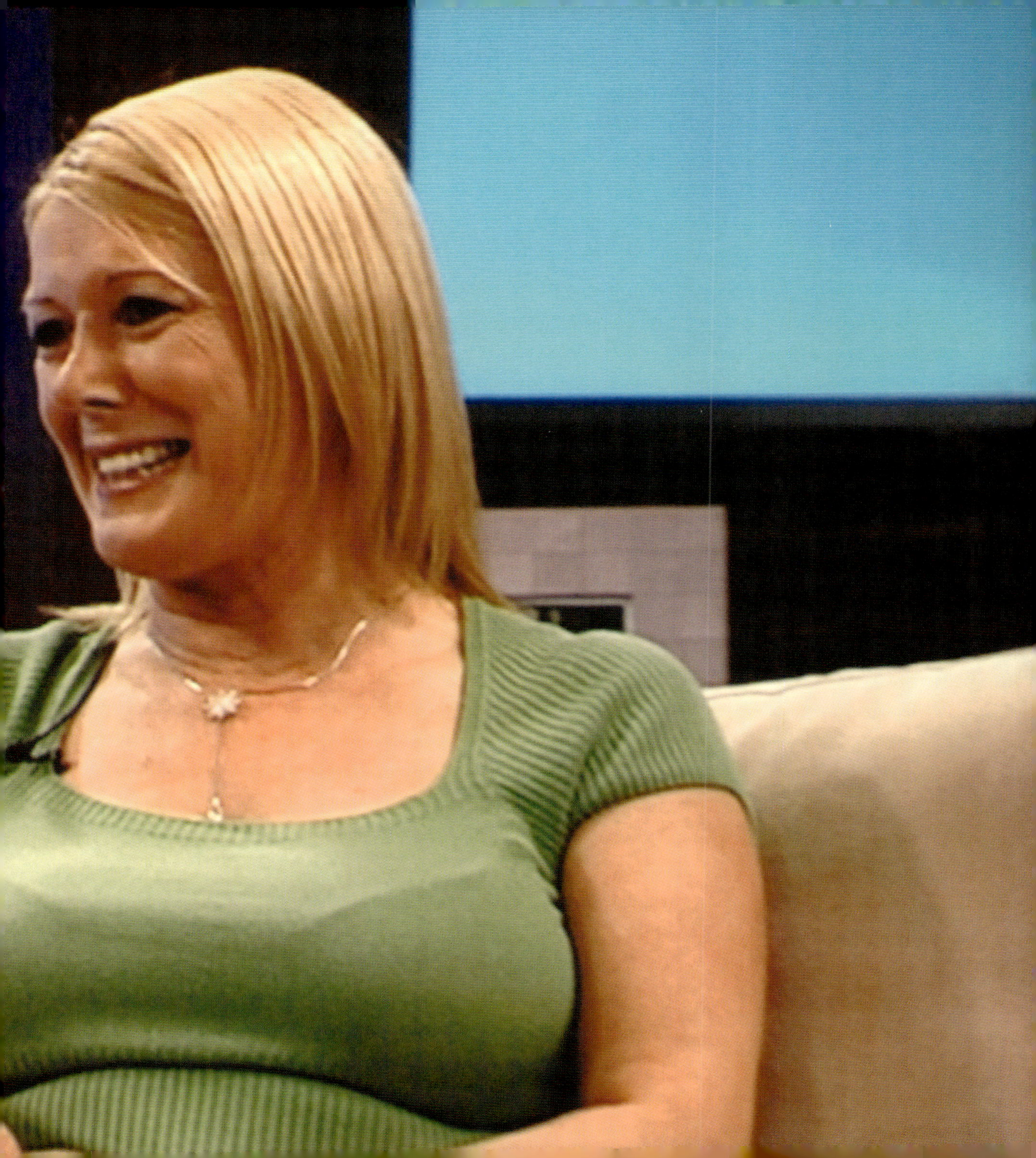

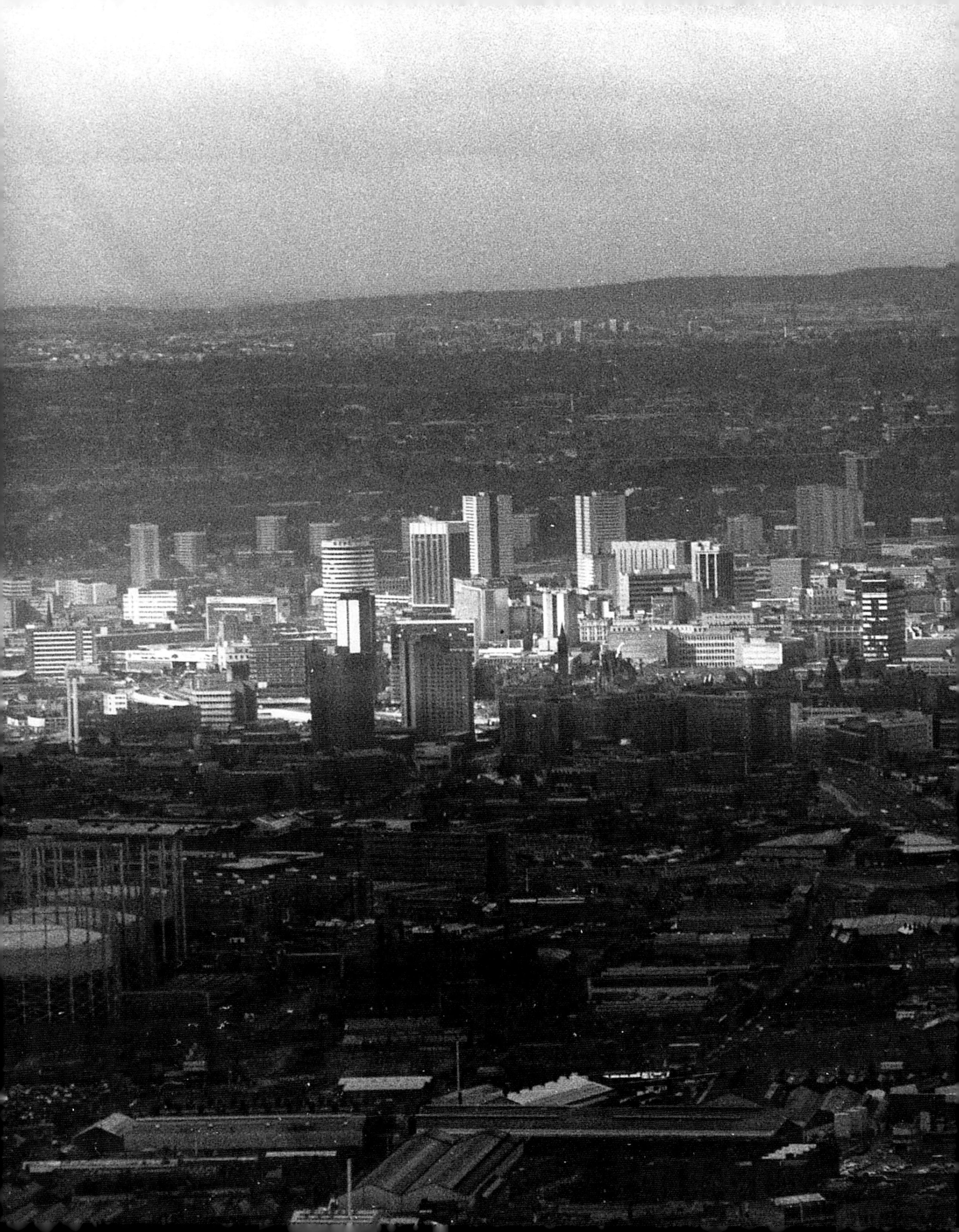

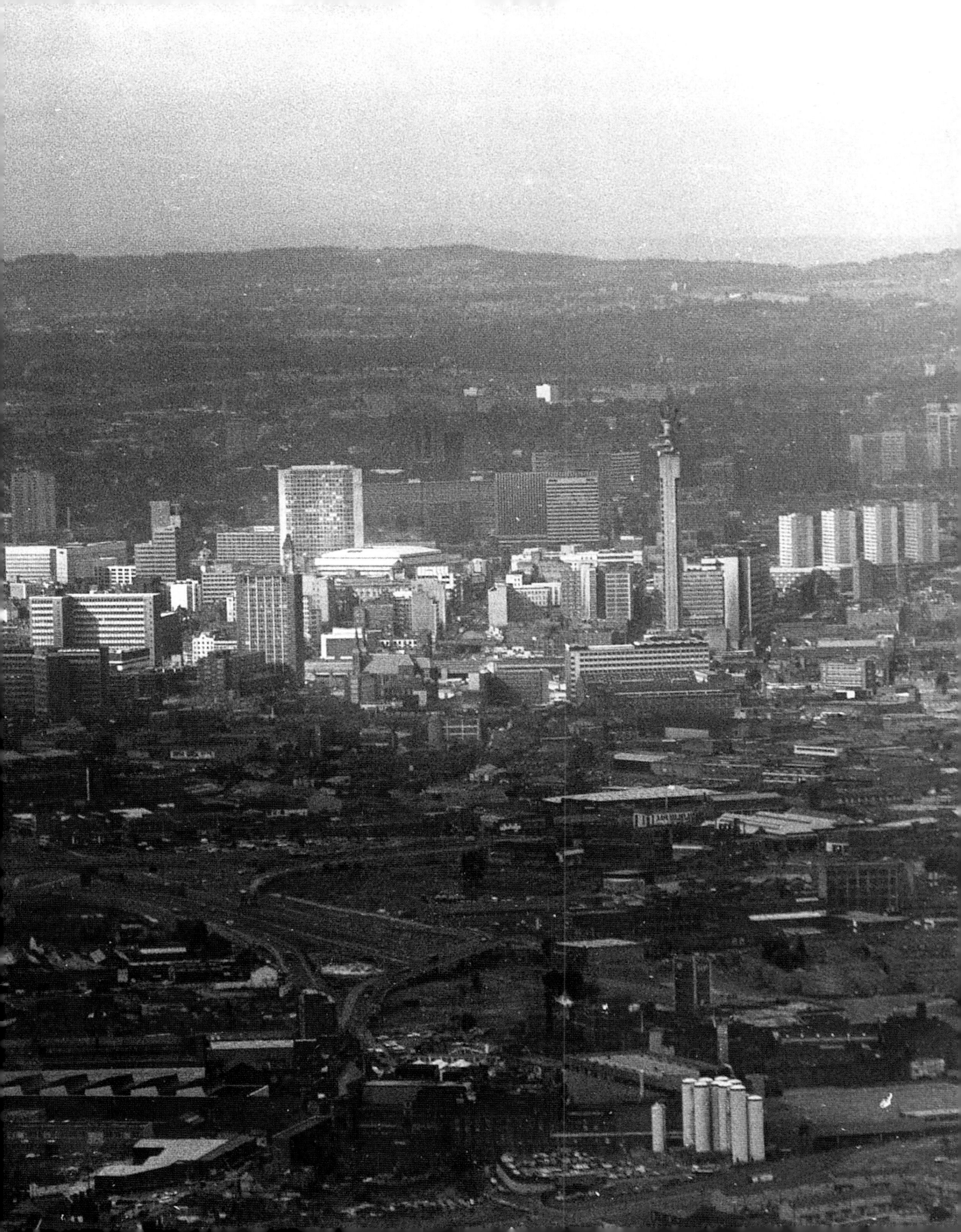

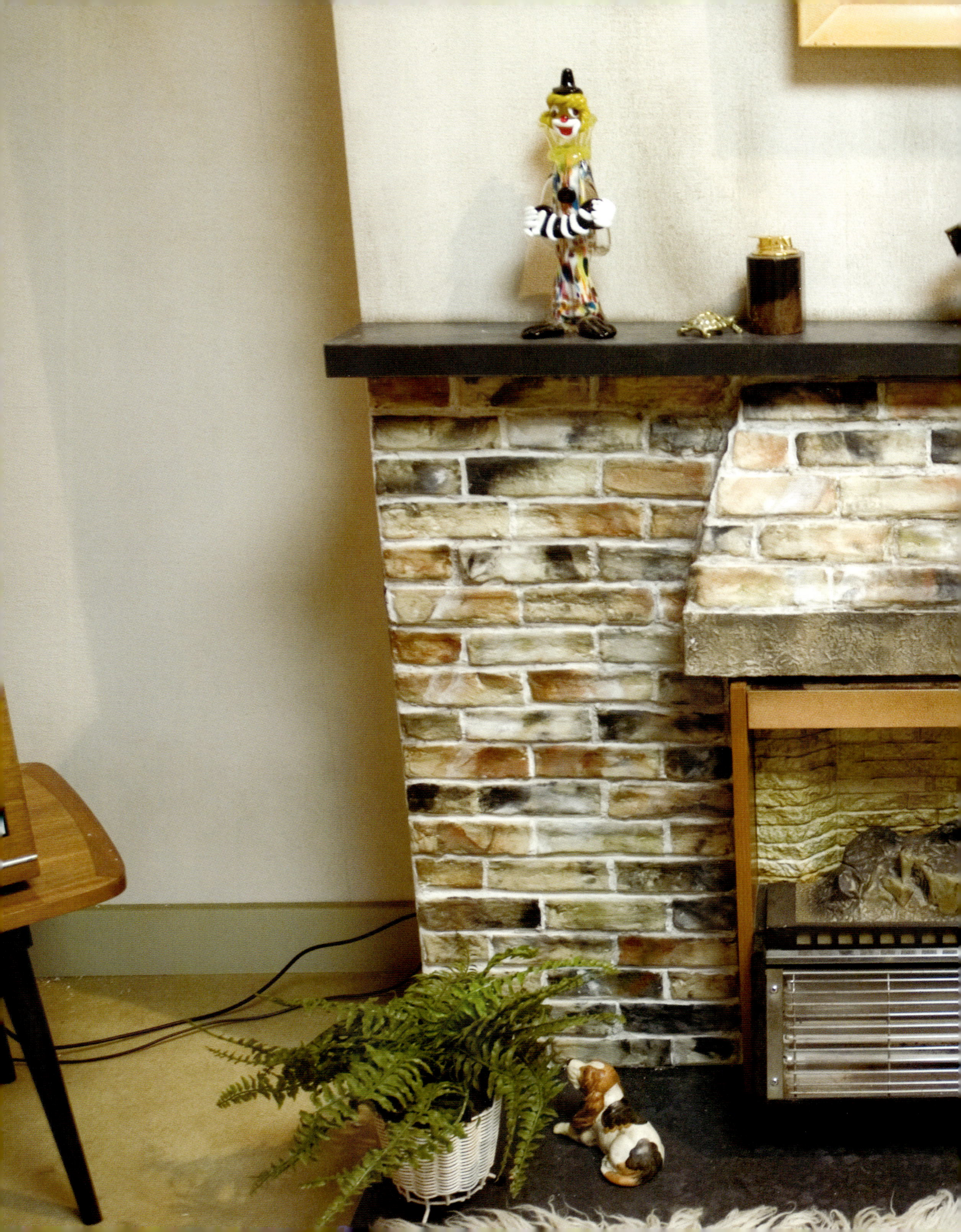

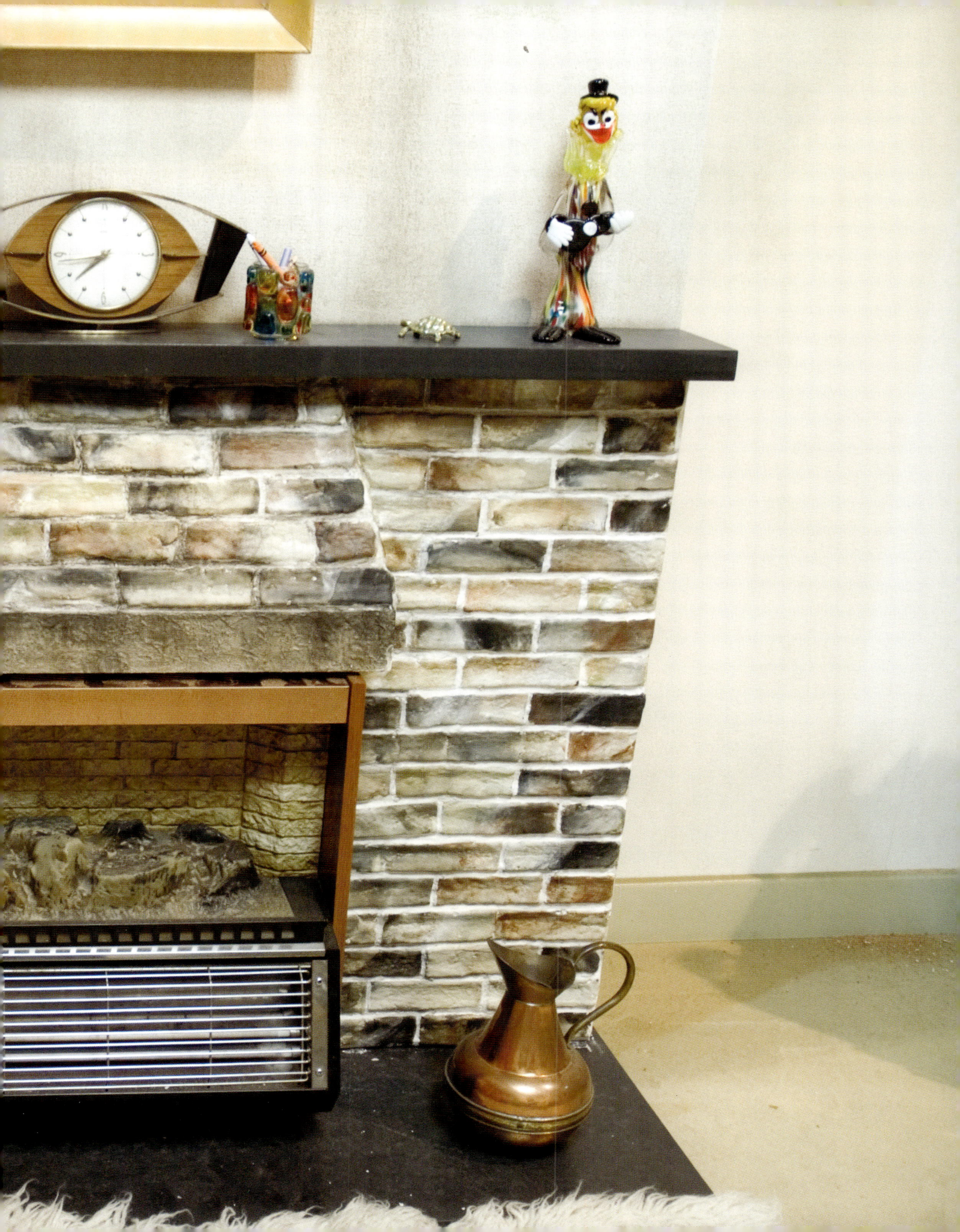

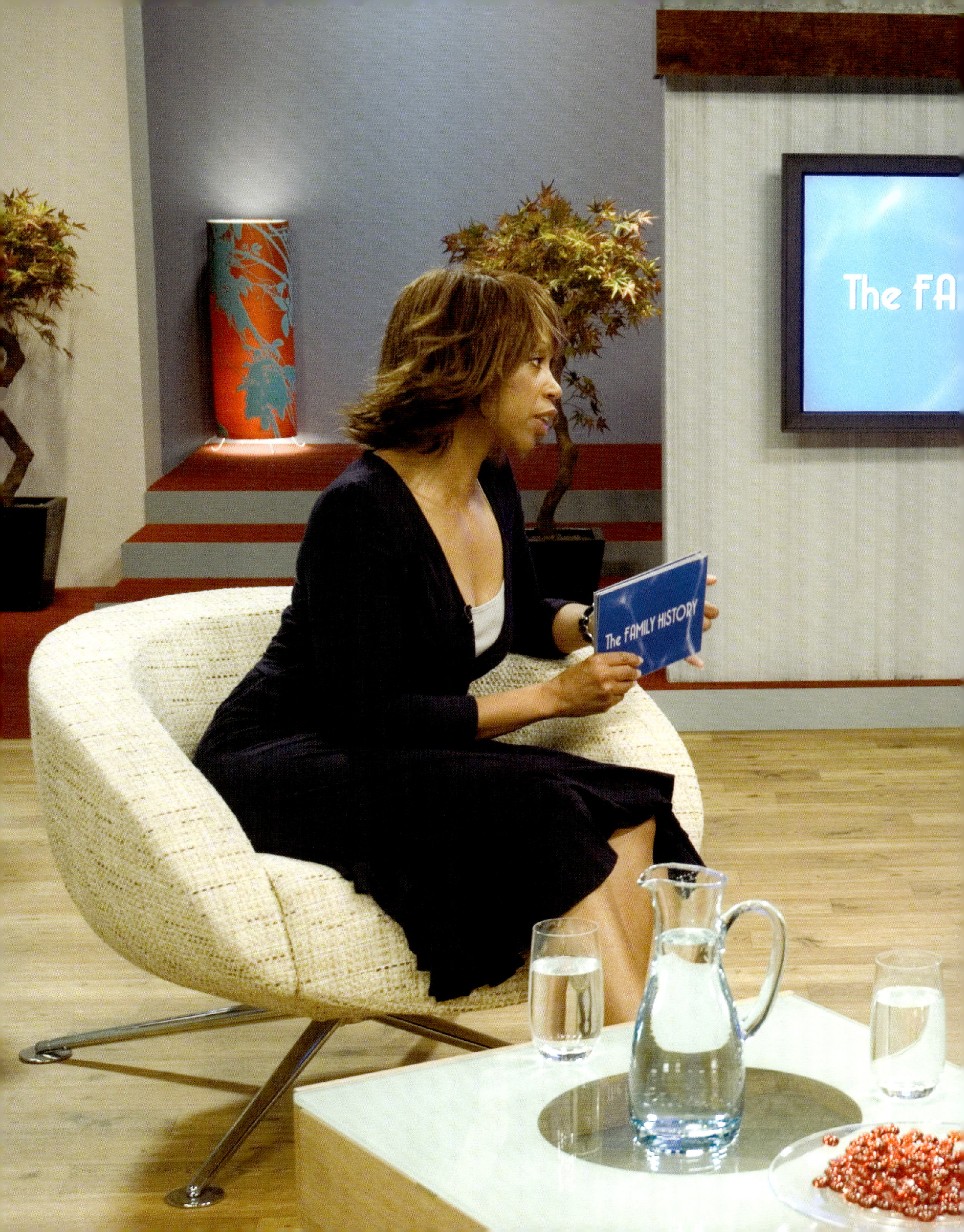

The FA
The FAMILY HISTORY

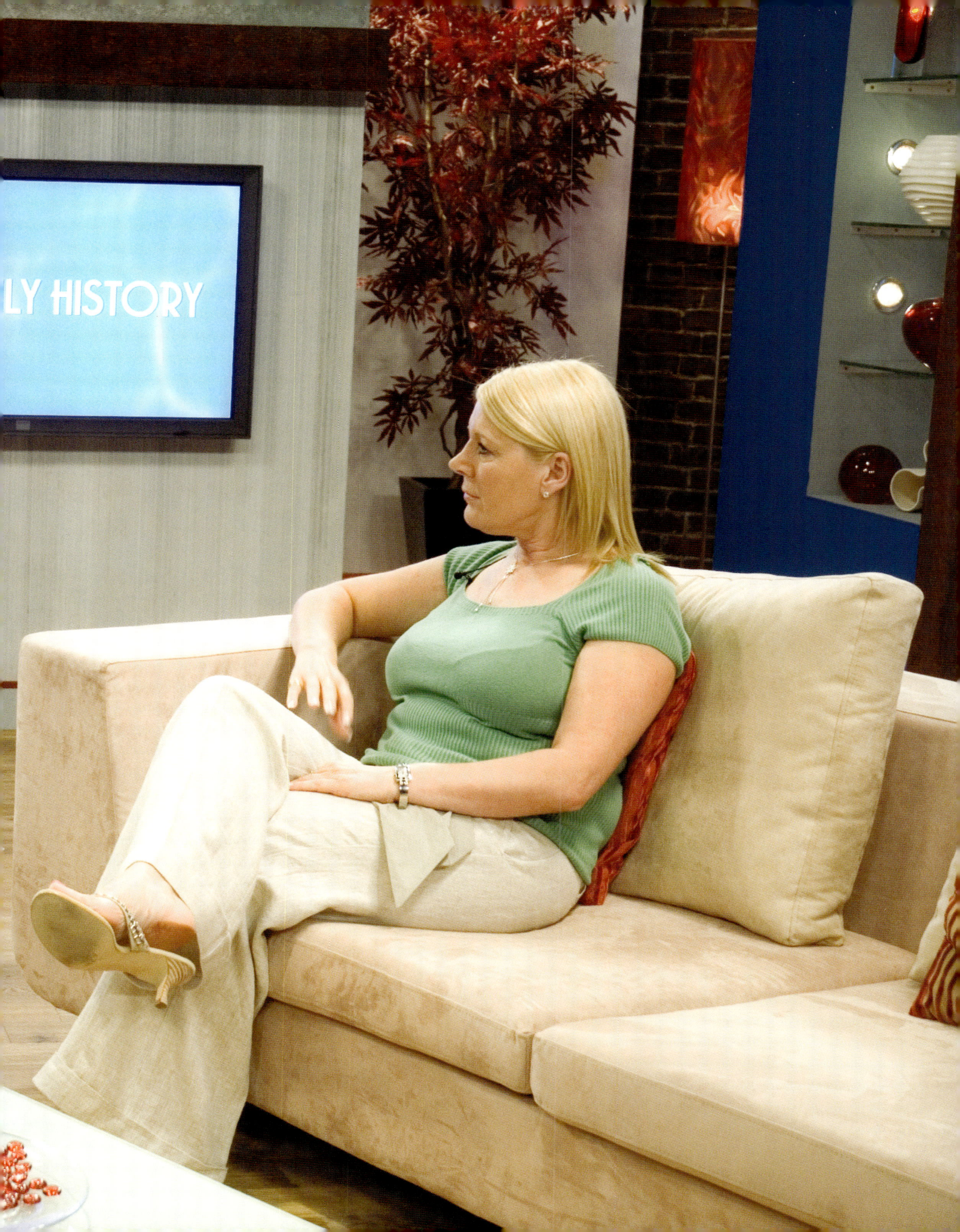
LY HISTORY

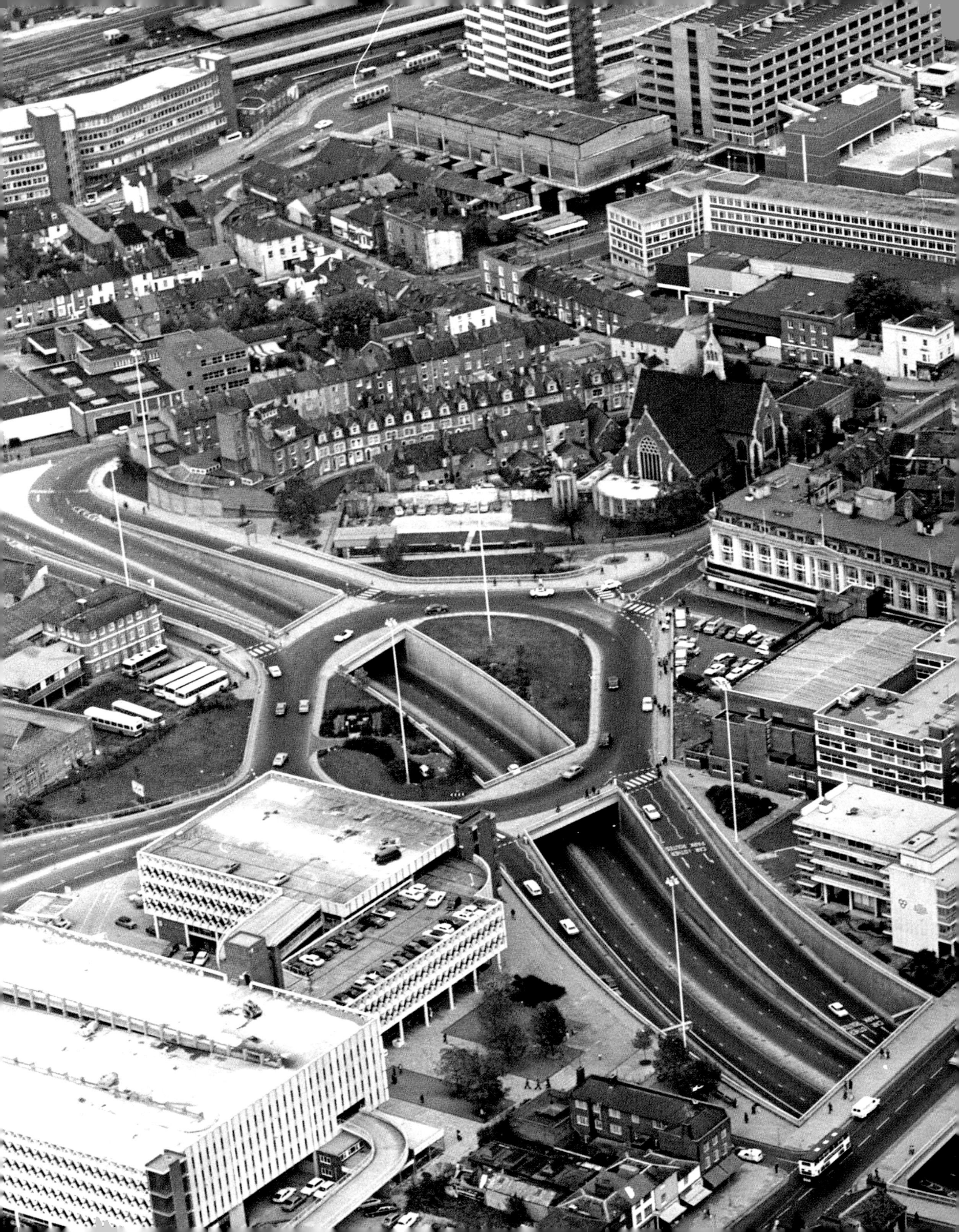

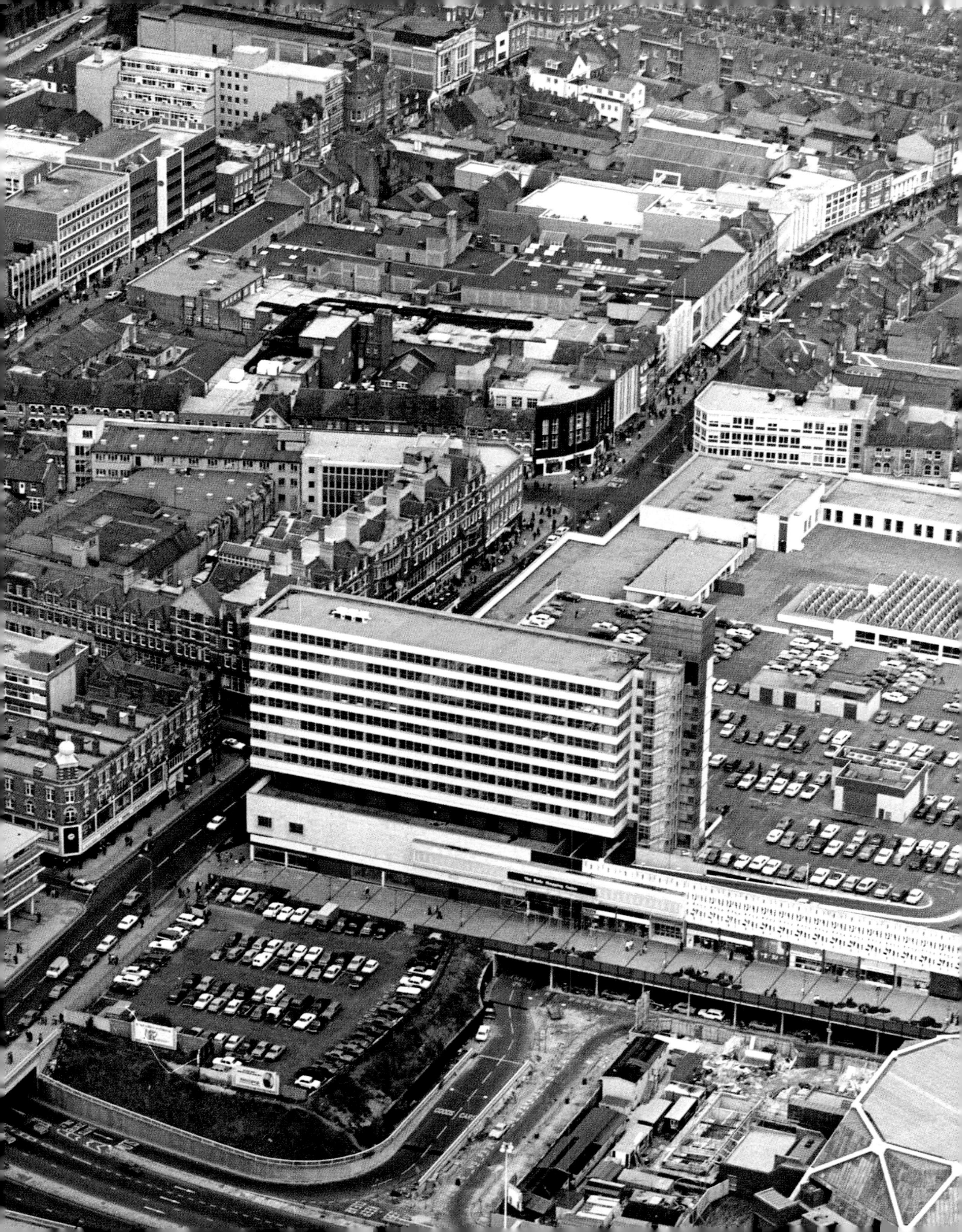

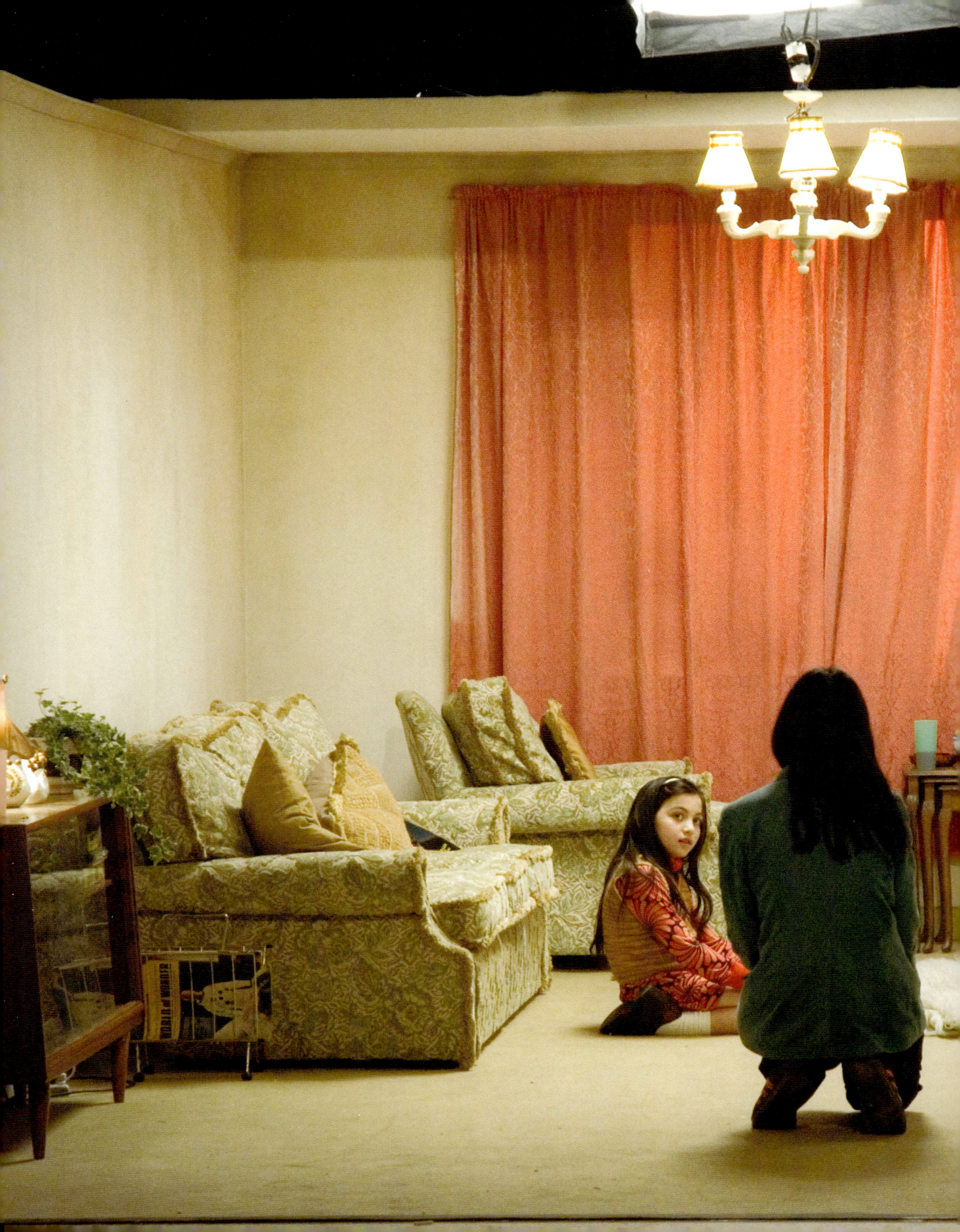

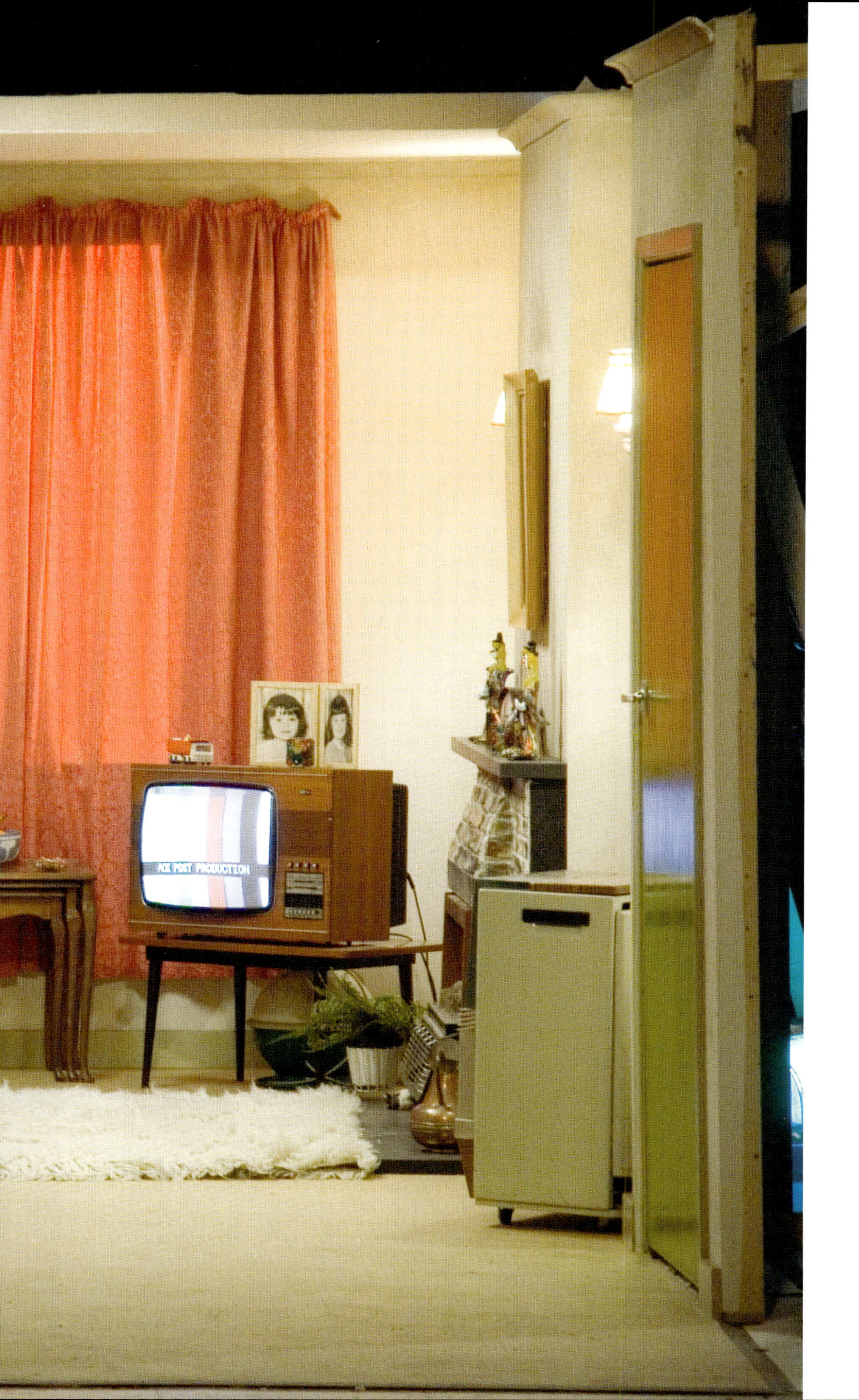
ACE POST PRODUCTION

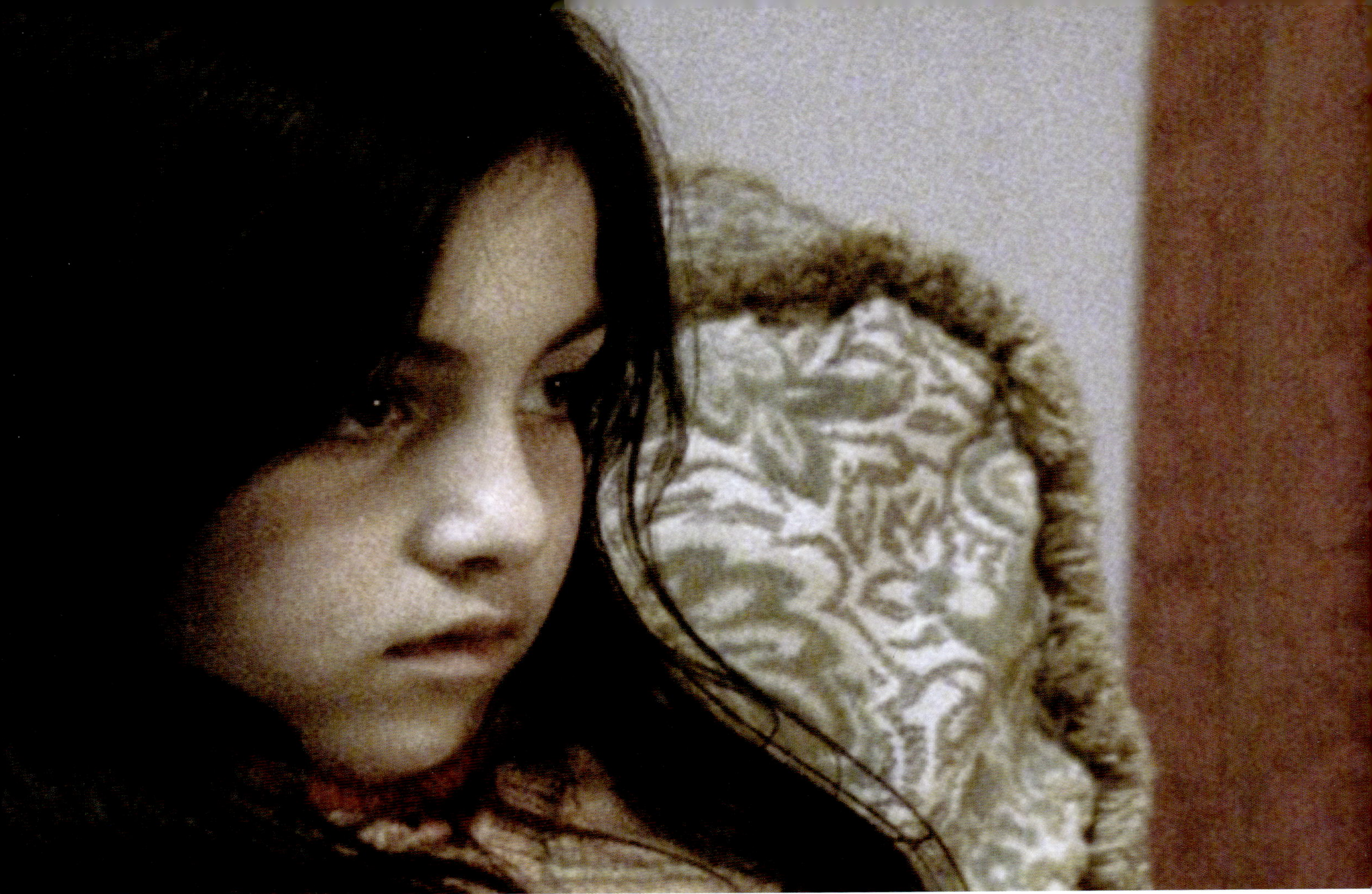

In Gillian Wearing's extended family of video and photographic portraits, 'Family History' occupies a particular pride of place. Easily her most ambitious project to date, this haunting and compelling two-screen installation gives intimate and complex expression to many of this highly original and provocative artist's longstanding interests and themes: the tell-tale gaps between public persona and private identity (and, by extension, the increasing blurring of everyday life and celebrity); the influence of television (and the media) on the popular imagination; and, last but not least, our continuing fascination with the representation of real life and its reflection in the distorting mirror of what has come to be known as reality television.

The starting point for the piece is Paul Watson's pioneering fly-on-the-wall documentary 'The Family', first broadcast in 1974 and one of the progenitors in this country of our current profusion of reality programming. Like its transatlantic cousin and nominal predecessor, 'An American Family', the series broke new ground in giving over unprecedented screen time to the previously unrepresented views and experiences of so-called ordinary people, moving beyond the occasional vox pop cameo or single issue-based documentary to take an intimate and lingering look at the everyday lives of an average family household.

Wearing's return to 'The Family' initiates a complex process of re-telling, recreation and reconstruction. At the heart of this story is Heather Wilkins, the youngest daughter of the Reading-based family which was the subject of the original BBC series, whose teenage years were marked out by the minor controversy and fleeting celebrity that accompanied her appearances on the programme.

Wearing's interest in the series (which influenced her greatly as an artist) has stayed with her since she first watched it as ten-year-old girl in her front room in Birmingham. Although the novelty of seeing an ordinary working-class family in its everyday domestic environment left a vivid impression, Wearing particularly identified with Heather (as a number of children who watched her may have done) as a kind of surrogate older sister, and also (in her mind) as a virtual televisual double of her school-friend, Christine.

'Family History' features a long interview with Heather Wilkins, which looks back at the personal (and cultural) impact of the programme, and reflects on the rich and busy arc of Heather's life since then. Conducted in the simulated home-from-home of a contemporary TV studio by daytime doyenne, Trisha Goddard, their conversation ranges from gossipy behind-the-scenes details to wider speculation about the influence of the series and the changes in British society over that time.

This interview, intercut with stand-out sequences from 'The Family', occupies only one of the two separate screens that make up the finished installation. Contrasting its brightly-lit TV-studio hyper-reality with nostalgic-cum-claustrophobic scenes from domestic life more typical of the 1970s is a series of shots of a young girl (a stand-in for the young Gillian Wearing), watching television in a mock-up of the front room of her former family home. Dressed in Seventies clothes (including an exact replica of one of Wearing's outfits from the period) and surrounded by Seventies paraphernalia, this young girl is utterly immersed in what she is viewing, but later turns to address the camera with her own thoughts and observations about what she has seen. Under the guise of a biographical survey of the life of Heather Wilkins, the piece also offers a partial auto-biographical portrait of Gillian Wearing herself, as a product of the self-same era, and as one of the comparatively few contemporary artists whose work has engaged with the power and the universality of television as a popular cultural form.

'Family History' has originated as part of a close collaboration between Film and Video Umbrella, Artists in the City, in Reading, and Ikon Gallery, in Birmingham. As well as revisiting the points of origin of the piece itself, that partnership has been of pivotal importance with regard to exhibiting the finished work in the two locations. In both Reading and Birmingham, 'Family History' has been shown, not in conventional gallery spaces, but in offsite domestic settings; ones, moreover, that illustrate the extent to which these two, strikingly similar, urban centres have changed since the 1970s. In the Forbury Apartments in Reading, and in Brindley House in Birmingham, Artists in the City and Ikon Gallery have secured the use of 'show home' apartments in newly regenerated parts of the city, in which the piece has been skillfully, and resonantly, installed. Situated high above the urban landscape, these re-developed sites, flagging an aspirational lifestyle into which families no longer appear to fit, add their own extra context to the piece.

As part of the wider collaboration that always distinguishes a project of this magnitude, Maureen Paley has lent significant support, facilitating a further staging of the piece at her gallery in London, and contributing generously towards this publication. We would also like to thank the Artist's Moving Image Network at Film London for additional assistance towards the book, and towards the production of the work itself. Finally, our thanks go to Gillian Wearing for the energy and dedication she has brought to all aspects of this project and for her equally strong personal investment in this accompanying publication.

STEVEN BODE
Film and Video Umbrella
JENI WALWIN
Artists in the City
JONATHAN WATKINS
Ikon Gallery

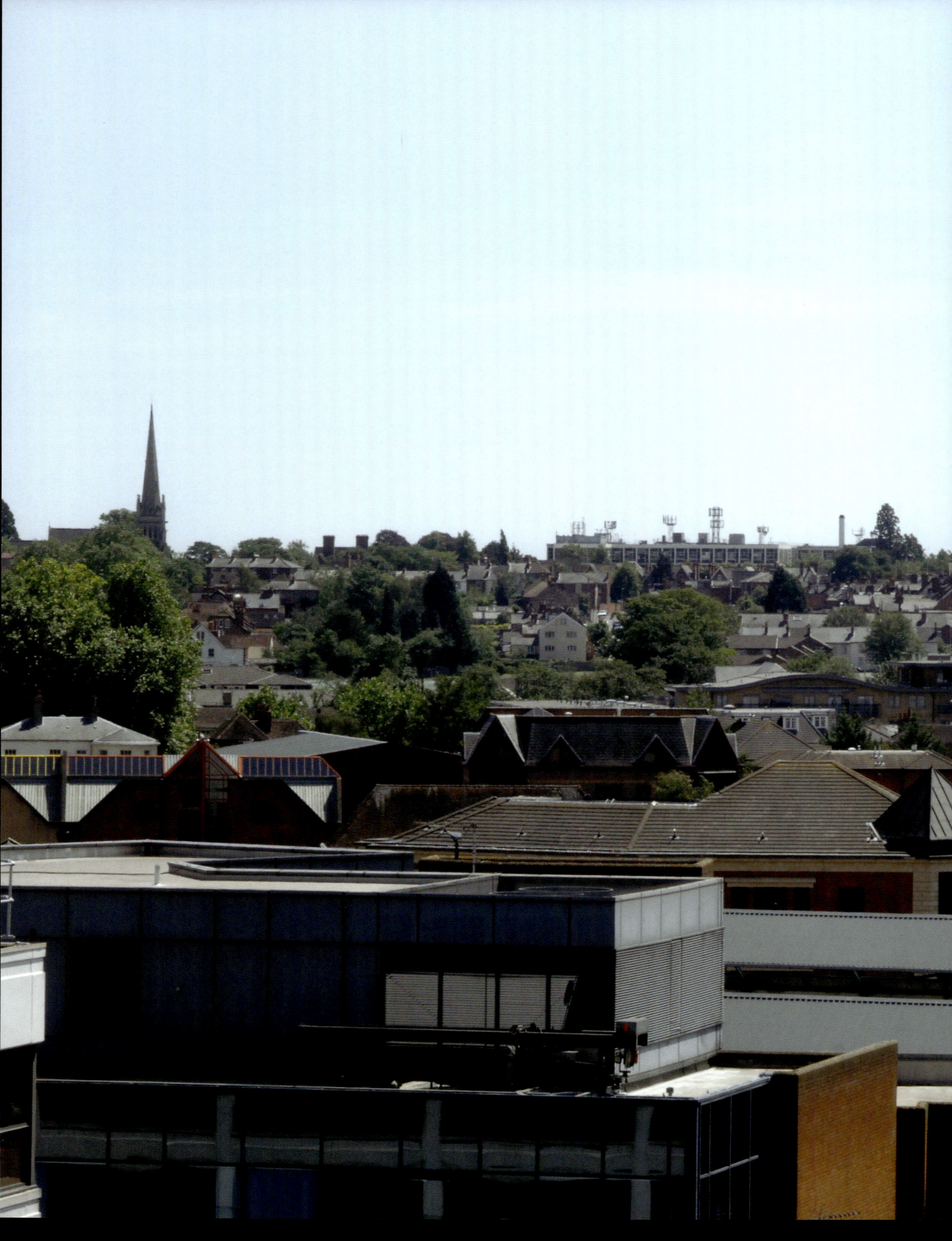

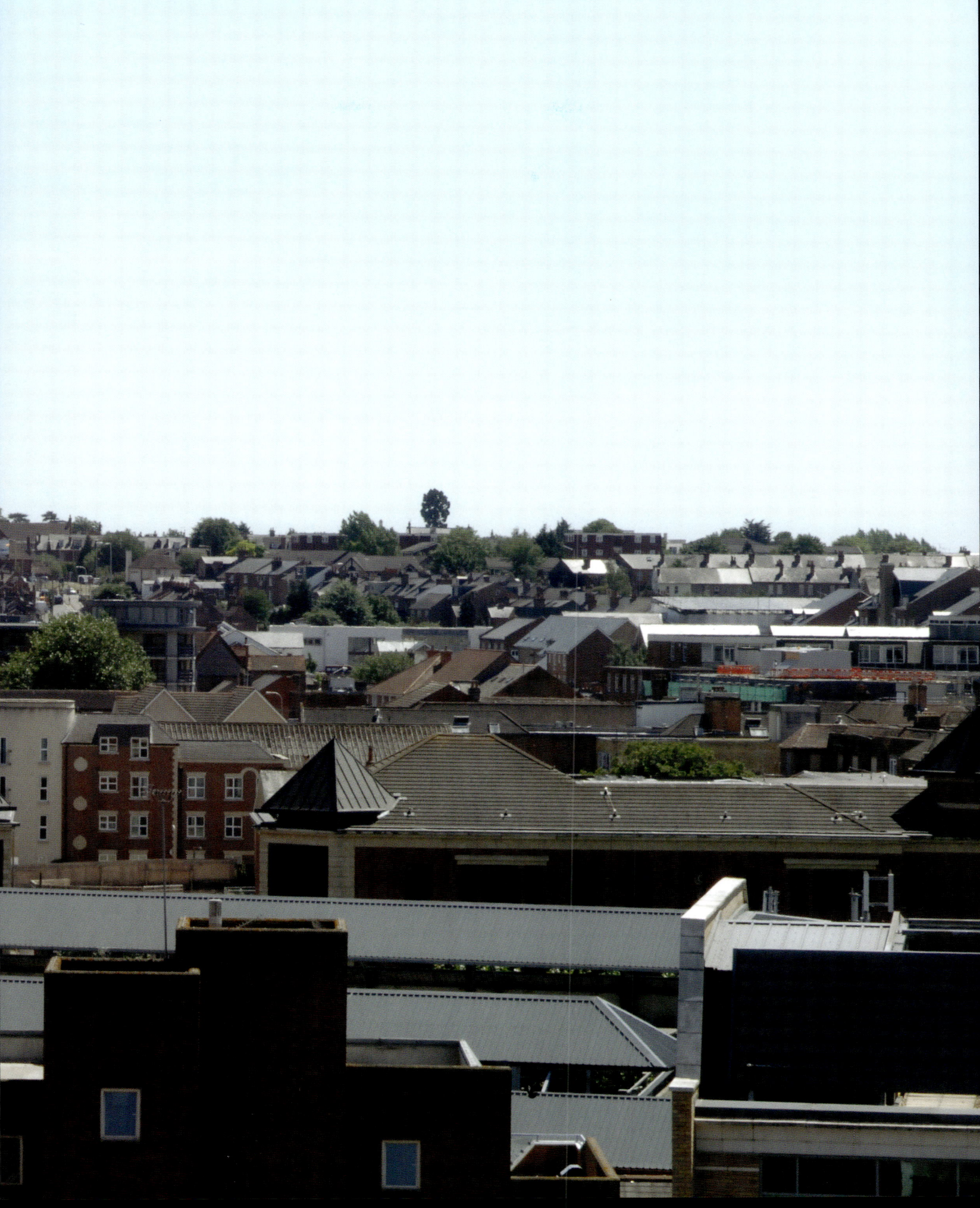

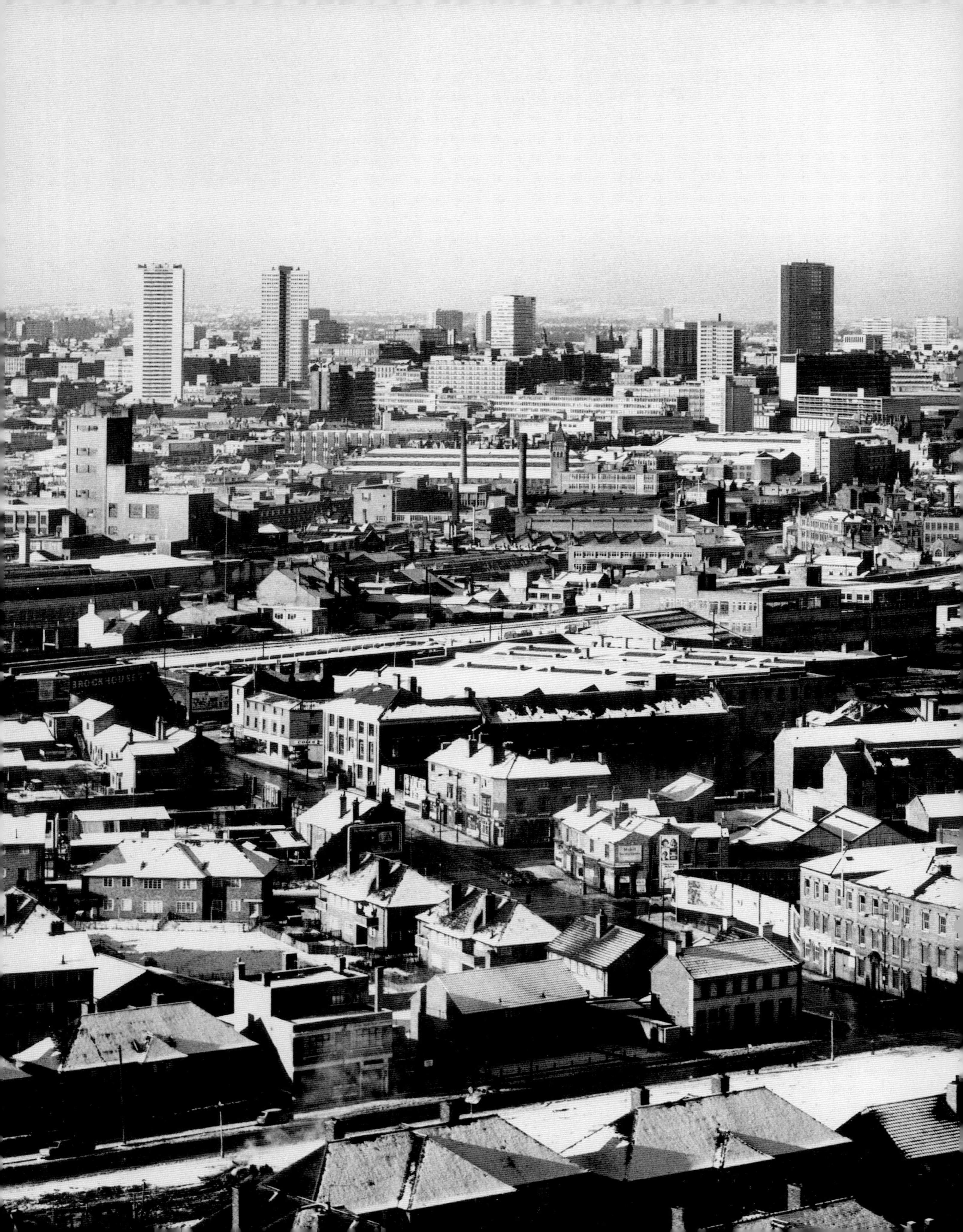

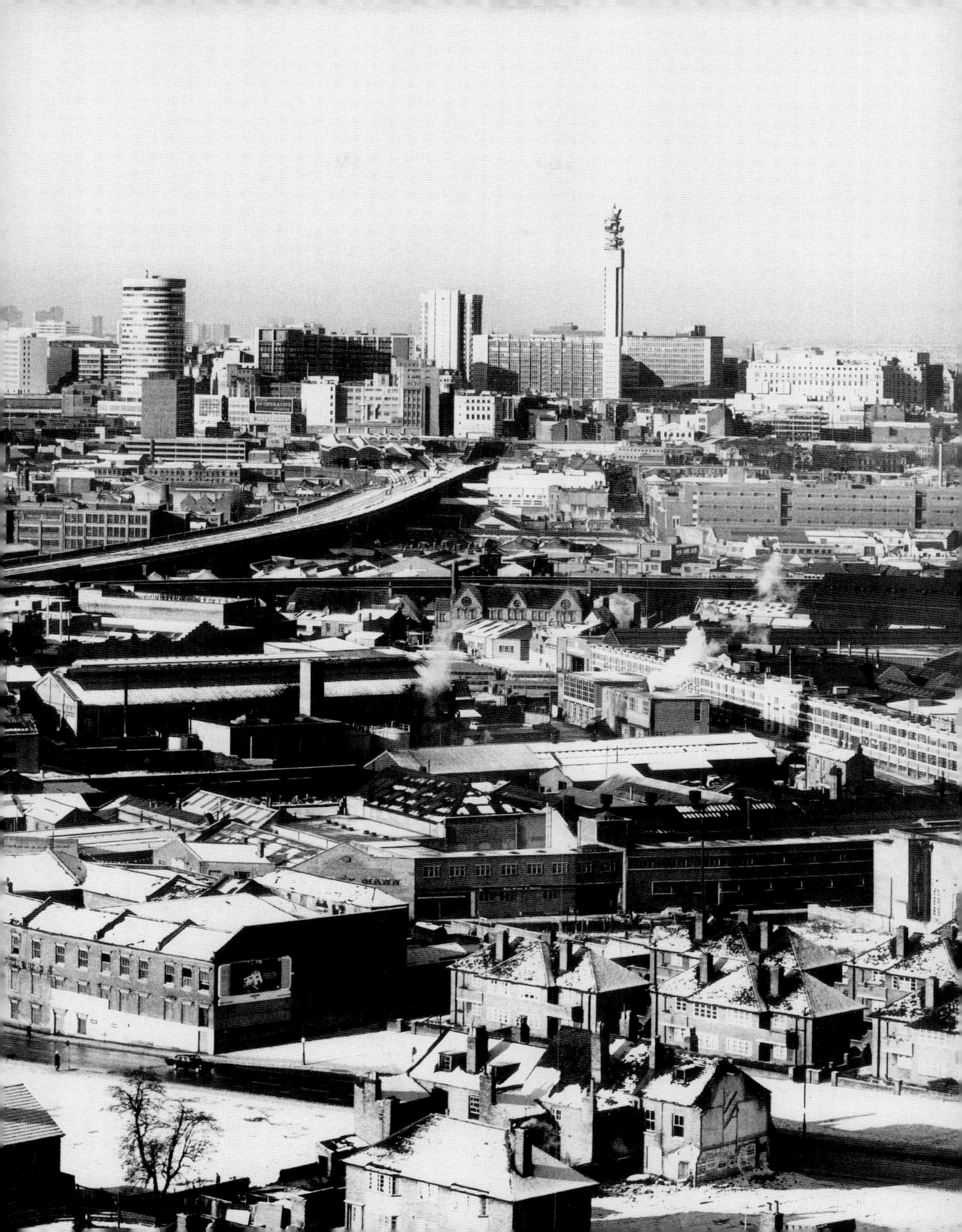

TV FAMILY WILL BE WED TOMORROW

FINISHING TOUCH

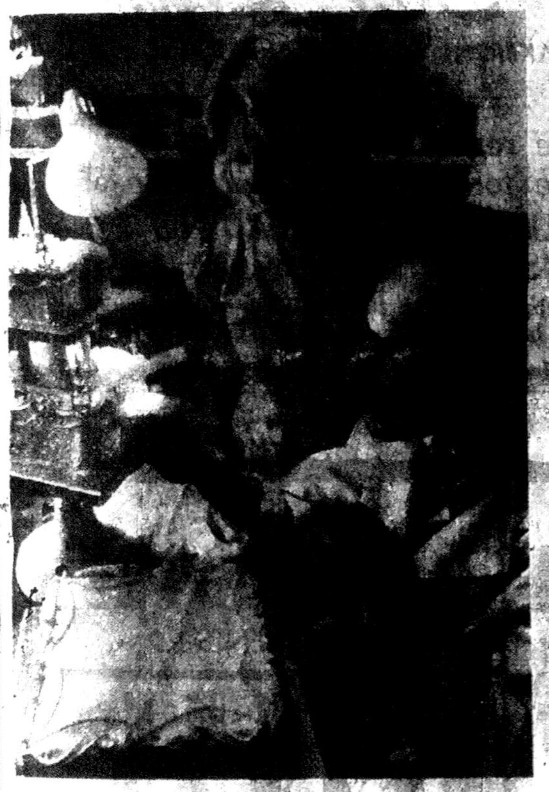

During her lunch-hour yesterday Marian popped in to watch Mr. Harry Parslow, of Table Dainties, putting the finishing touches to her three-tier wedding cake.

AND THIS IS HOW SHE WILL LOOK

MARIAN'S dress, a London creation, has been borrowed from a friend of her mother whose daughter was married recently.

Made of corded silk it has a high neckline, long sleeves and a train made of lace. The net veil has trimmed floral shaped edges, and is topped by a flowered head-dress.

She will carry a bouquet of white carnations and red roses.

Something old, something new . . . the superstition is not being followed.

Old — a lace handkerchief that belonged to her grandmother; new — accessories; borrowed — the wedding dress; blue — Marian was keeping this a secret.

Tom has a three-piece suit, grey-blue with herringbone stripes; an orange shirt with matching tie.

The bridesmaid, Heather, will be wearing an empire line dress in cream with green floral trimmings and will carry a bouquet of pink and white carnations.

Christopher, the page boy, will wear a white silk shirt and black trousers.

HASTINGS and THANET

STOM AND MARIAN

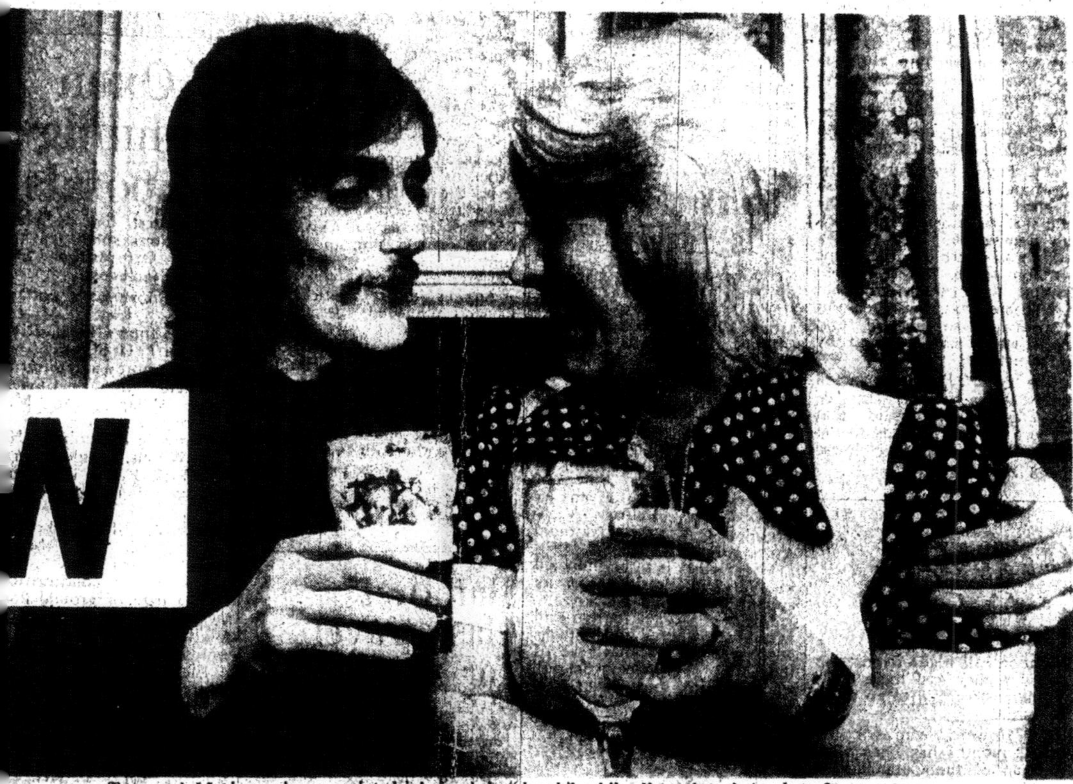

Tom and Marian enjoy a quiet drink in their "local" while discussing their plans for tomorrow.

N 'ORDINARY OCCASION' WHICH THE NATION WILL WATCH

VE them or not — it still be THEIR day orrow.

m Delmes and Marian kins, of BBC televi-'s "The Family" are ing married at Whitley l Methodist Church, a ding that will eventu-ally be seen by the millions of viewers who watch the programme.

Tomorrow's ceremony will be a family affair; about eighty relatives and friends will be at the church and afterwards at the reception at a near-by public house. The only unusual guests will be the television team who are filming the series which has attracted so much comment.

This week, in an exclusive interview, the couple revealed the wedding plans and some of their hopes for the future.

The wedding was naturally uppermost in their thoughts. They want, and have planned, an ordinary occasion, the sort of wedding that most young couples enjoy.

Tom would not admit to any nerves about the occasion, although Marian did. "I am not so much excited as worried," she said. "I won't be excited until Saturday morning. On Monday I first noticed I was starting to get nerves and I had to calm myself down by reading the Beano."

Tom, whose family live in Sheffield, came to Reading five years ago. He met Marian in a public house near her home about 18 months later.

"Our eyes met," said Marian. "He asked me for a birthday kiss; I didn't think it was his birthday. He walked me home—even then I fancied him like mad."

They were courting for 18 months before they moved into a flat together, but they had to move out 14 months later and it was then that Marian's mother offered them a home until they married.

"She did not want to see us split up. We were already living together and rather than see us break up she offered us a home. It shows what a wonderful person she is," said Tom.

"On the programme it may look as if she had been getting on at me and pushing me into marriage. The truth is we get on like a house on fire. She is a great woman and a great person."

The fact that Tom and Marian have been shown living together before marriage has offended some viewers.

But Tom believes it has helped them to understand each other better. "We are going into marriage with our eyes wide open. A lot of people say a lot of bad things about us, but Marian knows what I am like and I know what she is like. We know each others' bad habits.

"And I haven't been pushed into marriage. I want to get married. I want to be able to turn round and say 'That's my wife you are talking to.' It will make me feel good."

There was never a proper proposal, however. "He just took it for granted," said Marian. "He wants to get married, people who have watched us on television will see he is not the kind of man to do anything unless he really wants to."

It will be a white wedding. Marian stressed: "If I was pregnant I would not be getting married in white and I would not be getting married in church because I would feel hypo-critical."

They have been searching for a wedding date since Christmas. Once "The Family" were chosen for the television series they wanted their wedding to be televised.

"Only one other couple have had their wedding on television recently, after all," said Marian.

Marian had her hen party last night; Tom has his stag party tonight (Friday). He will be sticking to his normal drink, brown and mild.

Among those at the wedding will be Tom's family from Sheffield. He hopes his parents and three sisters will be able to make the trip, although his father has been ill and is still not certain if he will be able to travel. His brother will not be coming because he has a young baby.

Mr. Terry Wilkins will be giving his daughter away; Marian's sister Heather will be the bridesmaid, brother Christopher will be the page boy.

The best man is Mr. Roger Bishop, who was Tom's flat-mate when he first came to Reading.

Following the reception the couple will leave for a week's honeymoon by the sea and will return to their newly acquired flat in the centre of Reading.

They have some fine presents to help make their home— and one that gives them a lot of pleasure is an automatic washing machine, a gift fr the television crew, the from the cutting room and the BBC staff concerned the programme.

"They all clubbed toge and it really surprised us," Marian.

Added Tom: "It shows extent that all those invol in the programme are invol with us."

They have had other prises — telegrams and let from all over the country w ing them good luck.

Once they have settled d and saved up some money, plan to have a family.

"Circumstances won't al it yet, but children will c into it later," said Marian.

They will be sharing cooking — both can prep an excellent meal.

Tom's speciality is steak a mixed grill — only compl from Marian is that he le the kitchen in a mess.

PICTURES: NEIL LOFTHOUSE

THE MAN WHO WILL MARRY THEM

OFFICIATING at wedding will be the Minis of Whitley Hall Methoe Church, the Rev. E. Don Mason, who was Presid of the Reading and Dist Free Church Council, 1971–

Mr Walter Winch church organist for me years, will be at the organ

Mr Mason, whose decis to conduct the ceremony been criticised, was meet the couple last night for usual pre-wedding briefing

He has interviewed T and Marian on a number occasions since they asked to be married in chur

"They have faced up the sanctity of marriage, standards of speech and the importance of the stab of family life," he said. think they now fully res these things."

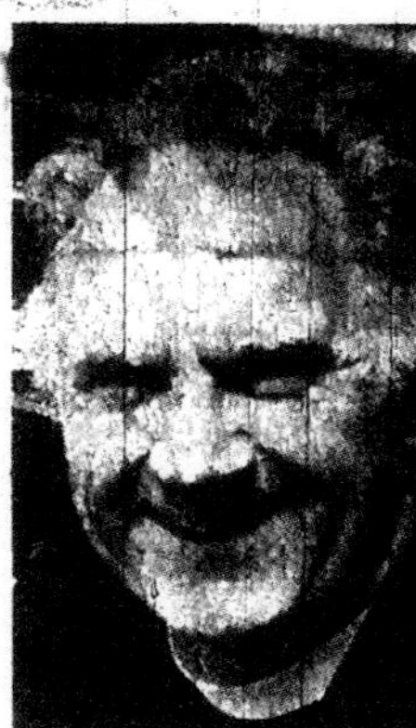

The Methodist Minist the Rev. E. Donald Mas who will conduct marriage ceremony.

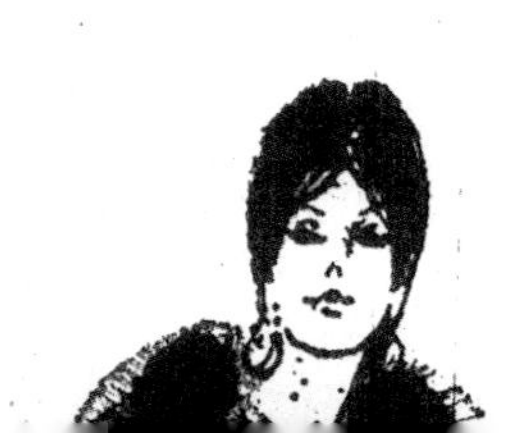

PROTECT YOUR PRECIOUS FURS

with

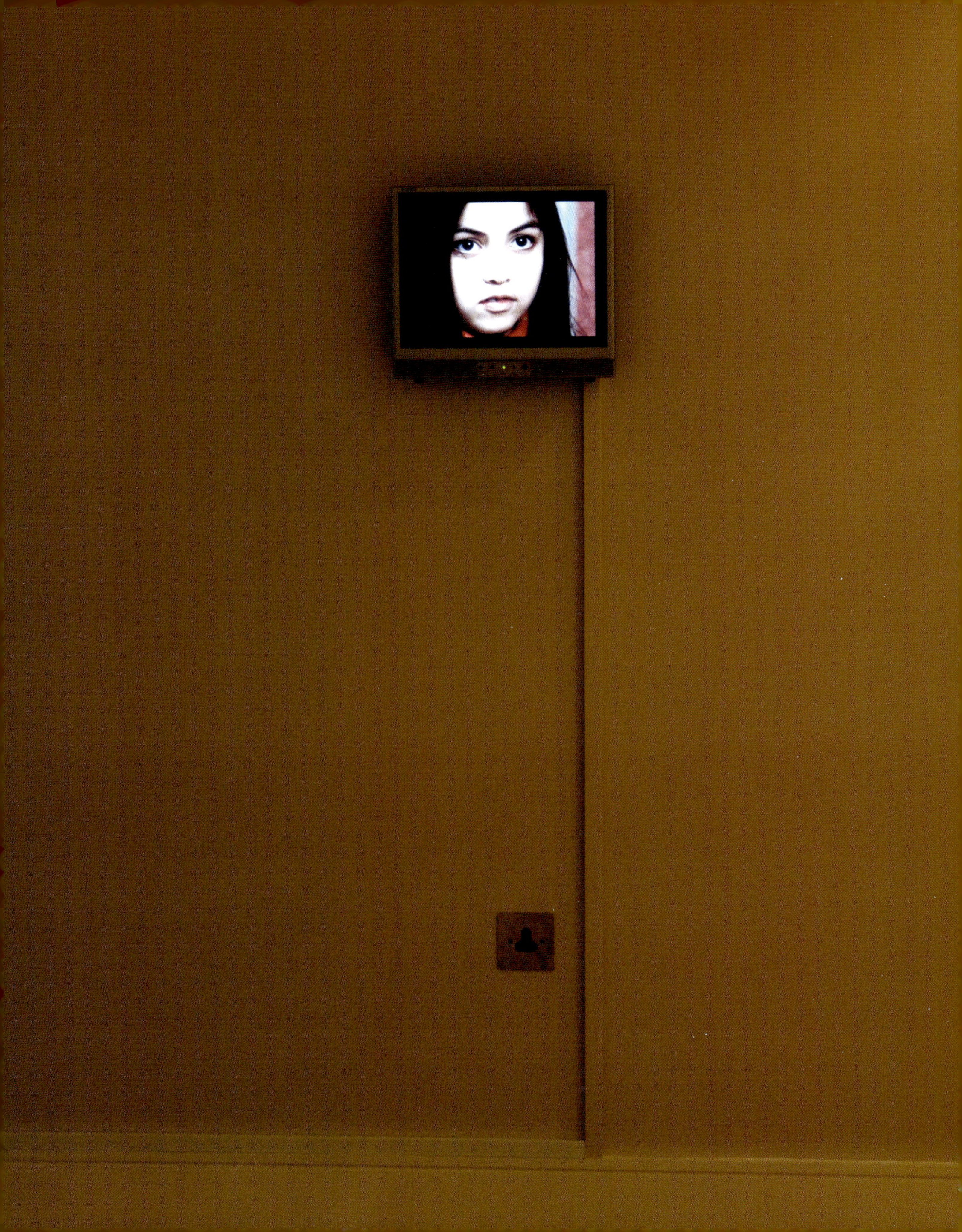

For many of us, the family is history; or, at least, a kind of history we find it easy to relate to. Faced with the abstract march of time, the family establishes a more personal point of reference; the lived lives of family members – parents, grandparents, great-grandparents – bringing history closer to home. The family takes the mystery out of history, lends it a human face. The family, and its place in history, has traditionally been a rich source of material for artists, and, more recently, for documentarists, working in cinema and on television. And, at a time when so much of the video that is shot throughout the world every day is devoted to camcorder mementoes of family life and family events, it is no surprise that artists at the forefront of the video medium should be increasingly fascinated by the family and what it represents.

One of the most popular programmes on television at the moment features celebrities tracing their family history. At the start of each genealogical journey, we rewind quickly through the last hundred years or so – moving back through a past that is marked out, era by era, by its different styles of family snapshot (today's digital images fading to Seventies Polaroids fading to early colour prints fading to hazy black and white). After a while, all the pictures go dark, and the only way to breathe life into a name on a page is to re-construct it; put yourself, or a part of yourself, into that person's place. It is not unlike when we close our eyes, in our efforts to recapture some of our earliest memories – experiences we guess to have been formative but which, no matter how hard we try and retrieve them, continue to elude us; that might almost have happened to somebody else. These phantoms of the past haunt the reality of the present, in the same way these unfathomable, instinctual forces inhabit our day-to-day personae. So much of what makes us, predates us. So much of what moves us, escapes us. It's all there in everyone – unconscious, unspoken, unexpressed. You just have to look out for the signs – although sometimes it needs someone to spell them out for us.

For some of us, watching intently during the dark days of the 1970s, 'The Family' was history; or, at least, a little bit of television history. A phenomenon at the time, Paul Watson's fly-on-the-wall documentary, screened over twelve episodes on BBC television between 3 April and 26 June 1974, seems even more of a landmark in retrospect. What's striking, thirty years on, is how innocent it all seems. The Wilkins family of Reading, chosen as the subjects of the series from a surprisingly small set of applicants, had no point of comparison for what they were doing, and, as became ever more apparent, no real inkling of what they might be letting themselves in for. Strange as it seems to us now, the family had no agent, and no one to handle their public relations, and were paid a relative pittance for their participation.

There was an innocence too, on the part of the audience, in accepting all that they saw as 'reality'. 'The Family' was considerably more real than anything people might have previously encountered (at least on television), and certainly made good on its promise to show life warts-and-all. Even so, it stopped some way short of the unlimited access that we have since grown used to, and was notably partial, and polemical, in its approach. While the limits of its scope, and the extent of its machinations, have become more obvious with hindsight, 'The Family' does offer the extraordinary spectacle of a genre inventing itself before our eyes – one of Watson's innovations was to put out the first programme before the filming for the series had been completed; heightening the sense of immediacy, and encouraging audience (and media) reaction.

The Wilkins family (husband and wife Terry and Margaret; younger children Heather and Christopher; older son Gary and daughter-in-law Karen; older daughter Marian and boyfriend but not-quite-yet-husband Tom) again seemed scarily unprepared for this. In a Britain that still looked up to the Royal

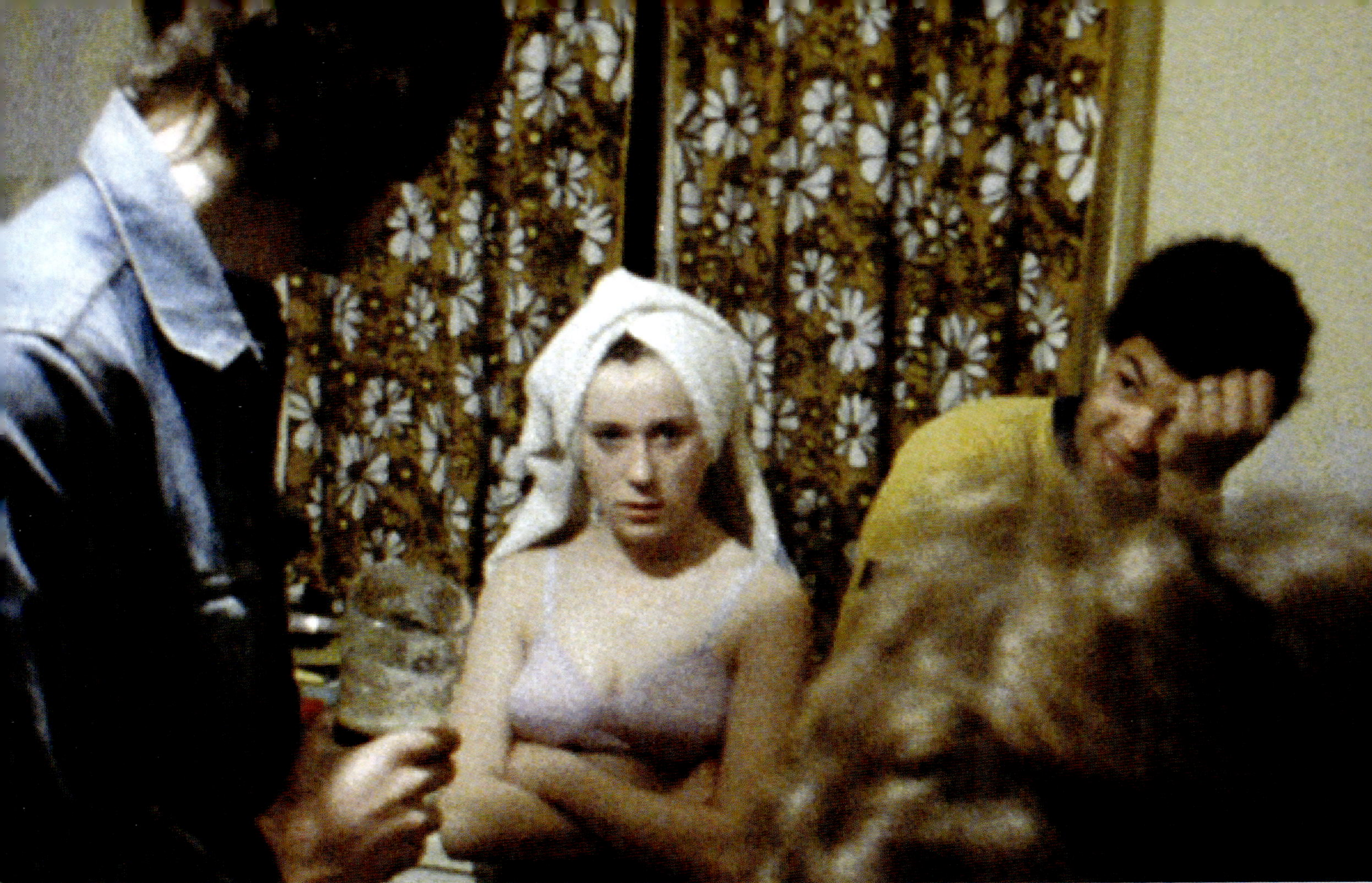

Family and hadn't yet hunkered down with the Royle Family, the Wilkins' everyday shouting and swearing was easily mistaken for boorishness, their easygoing scruffiness for slovenliness. If that wasn't enough to turn some people against them, Margaret's unusually laissez-faire decision to let Marian and Tom cohabit under the family roof was held up as a symbol of a steepening moral decline. When Margaret then chose the spotlight of the programme to confess to Christopher's uncertain parentage, the Wilkins became a walking headline: the family from hell. Having flouted a very English taboo that says you must never wash your dirty linen in public, they had gone one further by airing it on primetime. Little wonder that, in a few short weeks, they were hung out to dry in the tabloids.

It didn't take long, though, for the tide of opinion to turn. Like noisy newcomers moving into the sleepy cul-de-sac of the Seventies television schedules, the Wilkins provoked an early chorus of disapproval. Then people got used to them, and then, actually, quite fond of them. The media scrum at the wedding of Marian and Tom that closes the series with a deft soap opera flourish catches everyone by surprise – including the members of the public who turned out for it. (Having spent the last twelve weeks being made to feel part of the family, you can see why thousands of people might have felt that they had the grounds to invite themselves along to the happy event.) While 'The Family', for richer or for poorer, is largely responsible for spawning the cult of reality TV in the UK, this closing wedding scene stands out, too, as one of the key moments in a larger cultural trend: the coming-together of ordinary life and celebrity that would be so energetically consummated over the next few years.

For most of us, the family is destiny; or, at least, one of its big defining influences. Freud, who we should introduce into the story at this point, would have gone along with this; and Philip Larkin, following lugubriously in the analyst's melancholy wake, would have added another famous f-word to press the point home. Whatever they do to you, your Mum and Dad, it's never intentional: but it happens all the same... As always, in most of these cases, there are mitigating factors. Behind each and every anxious parent, trying to do the best for their kids, is a ghostly phalanx of earlier Mums and Dads, hovering at each others' shoulders, breathing down each others' necks; stretching back through the generations: all with their invisible baggage; their skeletons in their cupboards. Freud, in one of his more mordant turns of phrase, refers to this fumbled hand-me-down of our emotional DNA, with its seemingly irreparable faulty genes of Oedipal discord and conflict, as the 'family romance', an expression that carries an echo, in German, of the **familienroman**: the family novel, or family story. It is a story that carries on and on: a secret family history that you won't find in any public records, but whose complex genealogy is a mystery we are all still trying to solve.

For the Wilkins clan, 'The Family' was destiny; or, at least, their own individual interpretation of it. Margaret Wilkins, the bustling matriarch who dragged her not-wholly-reluctant brood from the privacy of their bedrooms into TV-land's hall of fame, talks of the night of the first BBC broadcast as the fulfilment of a dream. For other family members, the attention and notoriety they attracted was a millstone around their necks. Terry Wilkins and his future son-in-law Tom, in particular, grew increasingly unhappy with the

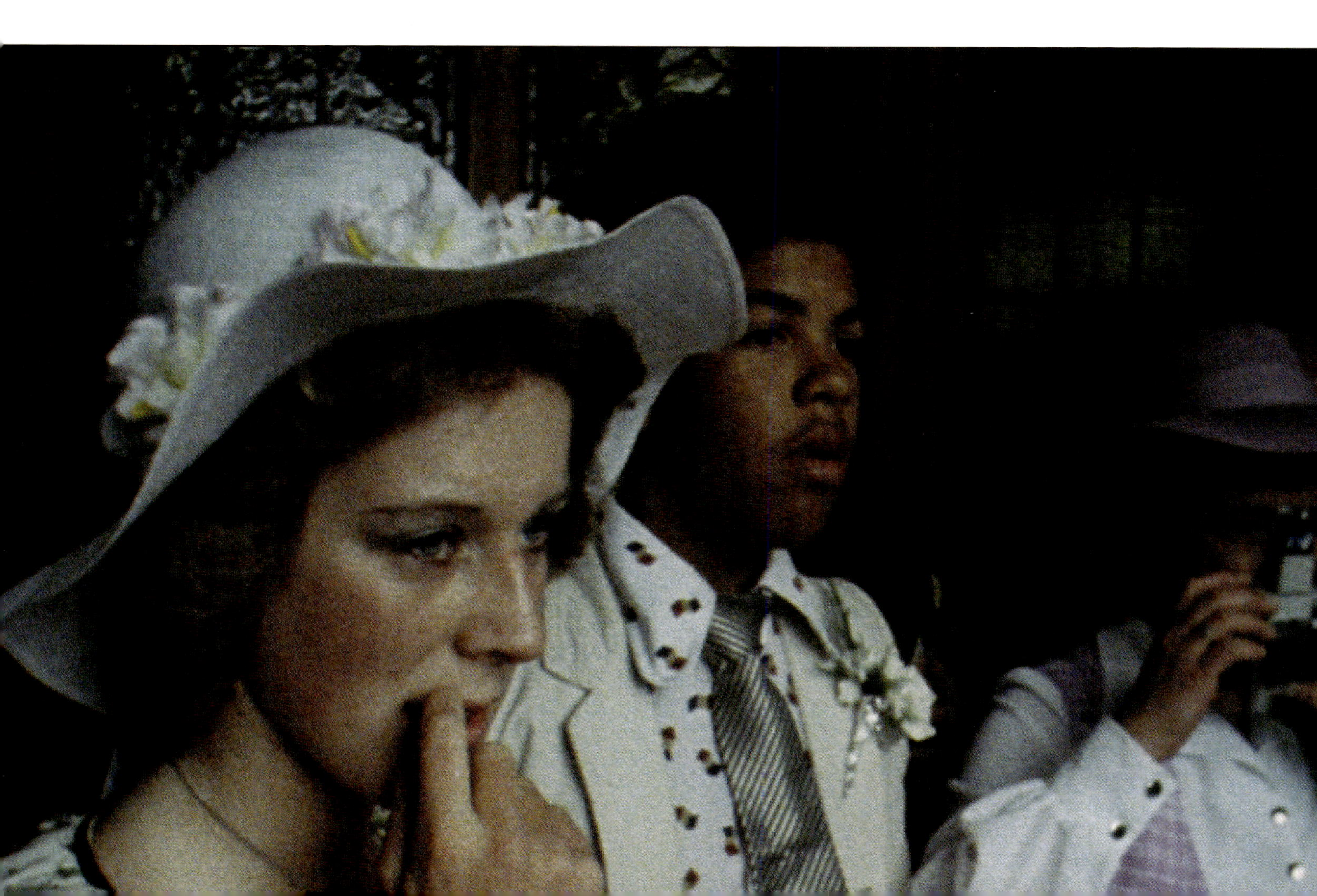

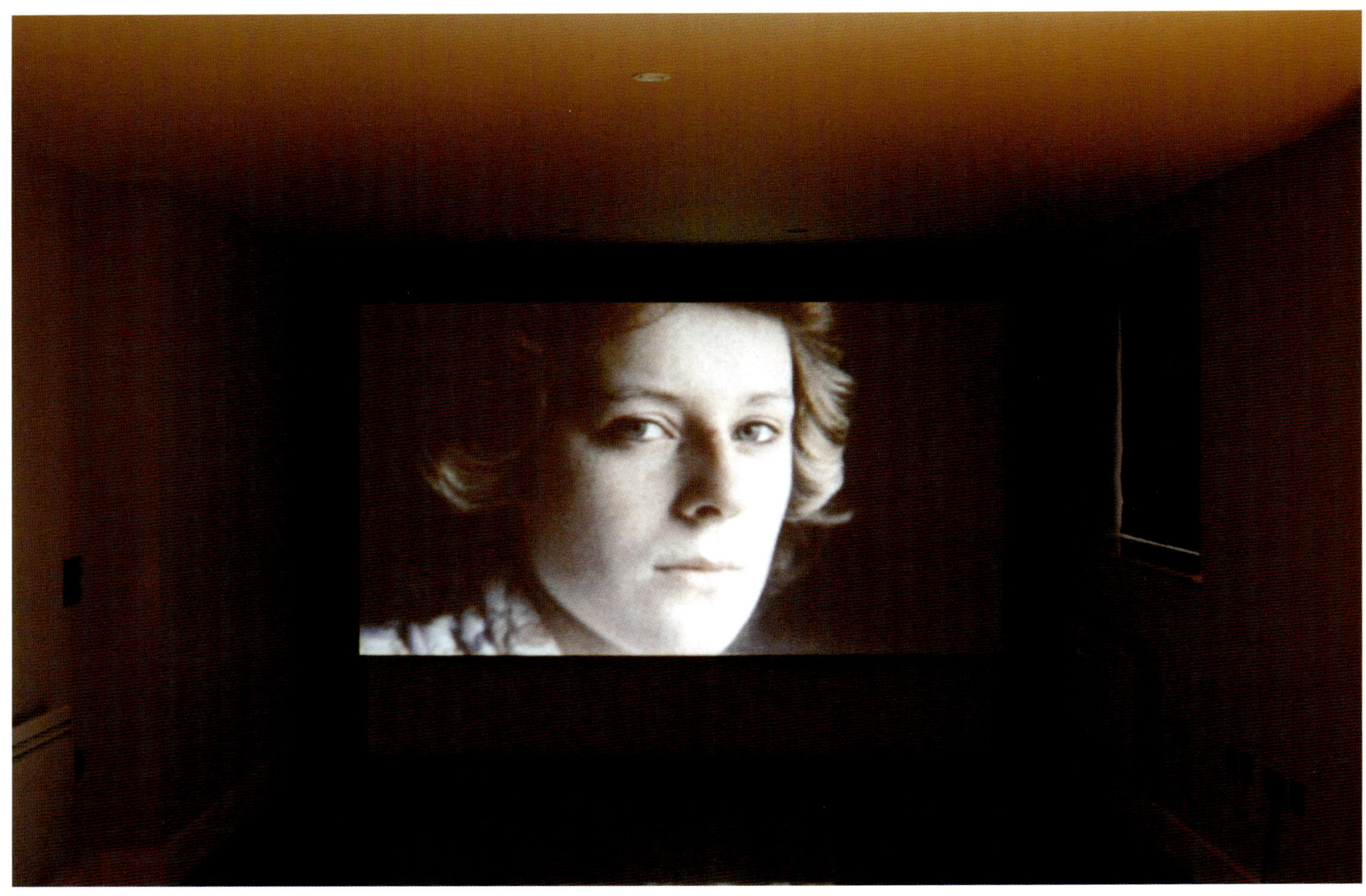

experience, not so much for the way they were represented but with the way that representation continued to dog them, and while plugging on gamely throughout the course of the series, have wanted little to do with the programme ever since. (Margaret and Terry separated a year or so after the series ended, and there has been no soap opera reconciliation… When TV researchers come calling, as they inevitably do, at the time of a key anniversary, or with an idea for a programme listing the One Hundred Best Documentaries, it is Margaret and her daughters who come out and chat for the cameras. The men are nowhere to be seen…)

Out of all of the Wilkins family, the person you would have expected to have been most affected by the fall-out from the series was Margaret and Terry's youngest daughter, Heather. A fifteen year old handed her fifteen minutes of fame, a feisty ingénue forced to grow up in public, Heather nonetheless emerges as one of the stars of the programme, her infectious mix of rebelliousness and vulnerability endearing her to the watching millions. There was no competitive element to 'The Family', of course, and while it seemed as if there were people in her own family circle who would have gladly had her thrown out of the house, the nation, lacking the requisite peak-rate phone-lines through which to register their allegiance, warmed to her, quietly, from a distance. Among them, 150 miles away in a suburb of Birmingham, was the ten-year-old Gillian Wearing, for whom Heather was a childhood icon and early role model; someone who, in manner, if not in actual appearance, was also a dead ringer for her best friend, Christine.

Judging by the long interview with Trisha Goddard that comprises the main part of Wearing's 'Family History', Heather has lost none of her former sparkle. Happy to trade gossipy confidences with the Queen of daytime TV, then subtly deflect anything she doesn't want to discuss, Heather is disarmingly poised and self-possessed. For someone whose life was so heavily encroached upon at such an apparently pivotal moment, she seems cheerily unaffected by the experience — although you can't help noticing that, somewhere along the way, she has turned into a highly polished media performer. A mother herself, although for much of that time a single parent, she has brought her own family into the world; a family which, from the way she describes it at the end of the interview, is very different, in its make-up and outlook, from the one she grew up in. If the Wilkins family (fractious, parochial, borderline bigoted) were all-too-typical of the straitened 1970s,

Heather and her children (mixed-race, precocious, independent) relay something of the wider horizons of the Britain of the early 21st century.

For a lot of us, the family is history; or, at least, the family as we thought we knew it. Already fragmenting from the seismic shifts of the Sixties and Seventies, the standard-issue nuclear family — of family mealtimes and family outings, of family viewing of family entertainment round a family-sized TV set — has become increasingly atomised; dispersed and diffused. Families always were a collection of individuals, but these days it is the individual that is the unit of currency, the force that makes its presence felt. If you want to see evidence of the declining pre-eminence of the family, you only have to look at the architecture around you. In places like Reading and Birmingham, whole swathes of once-populous streets, with their

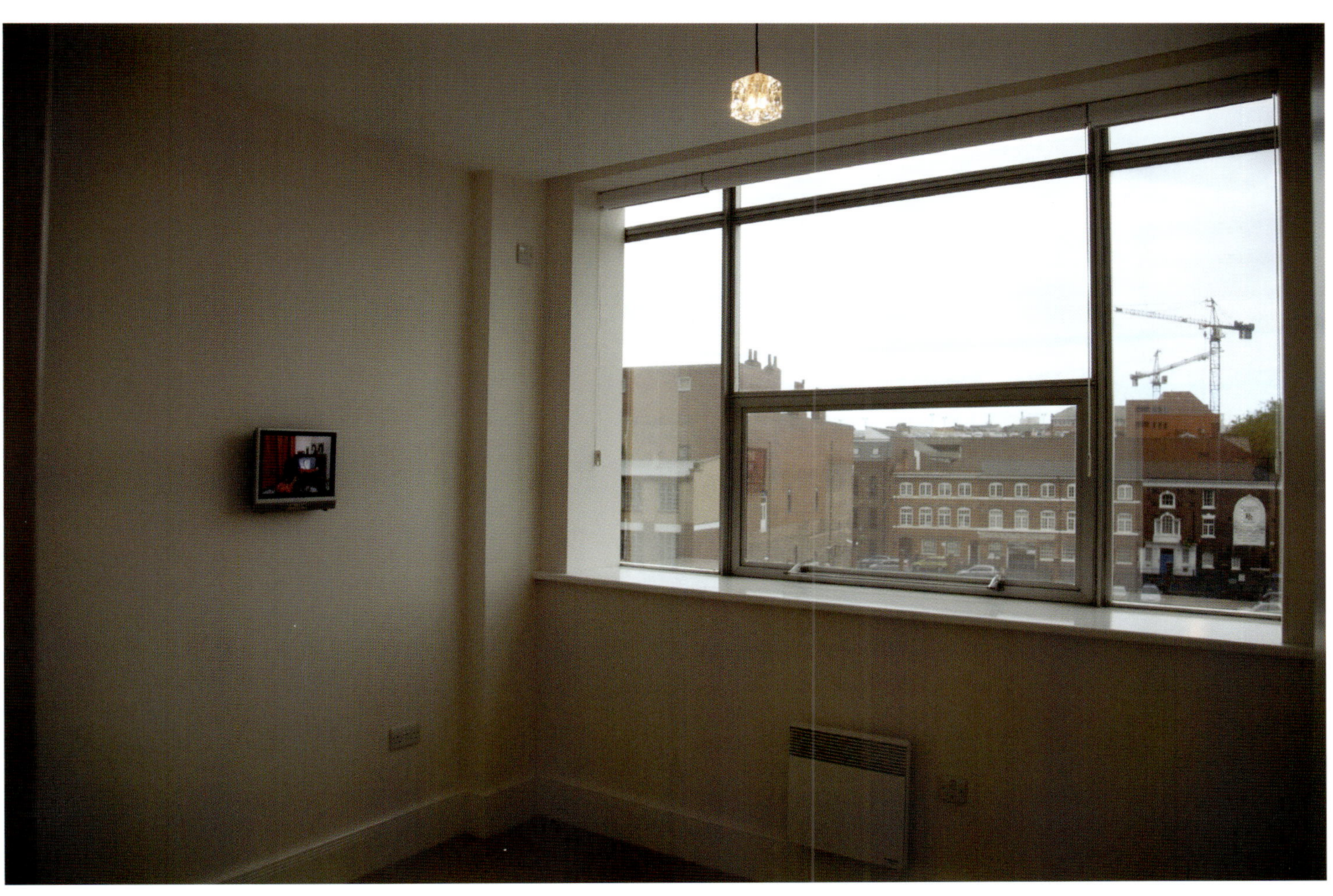

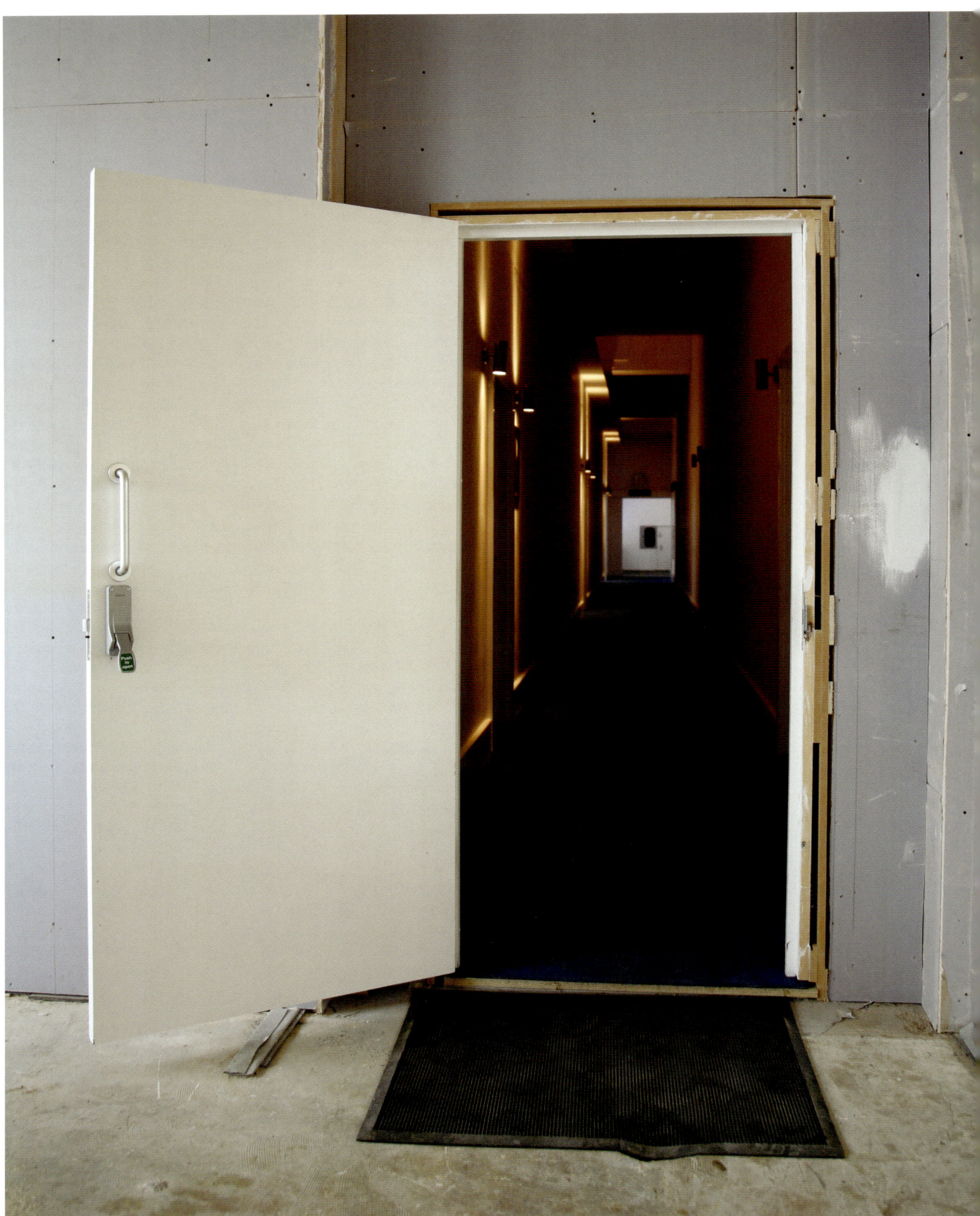

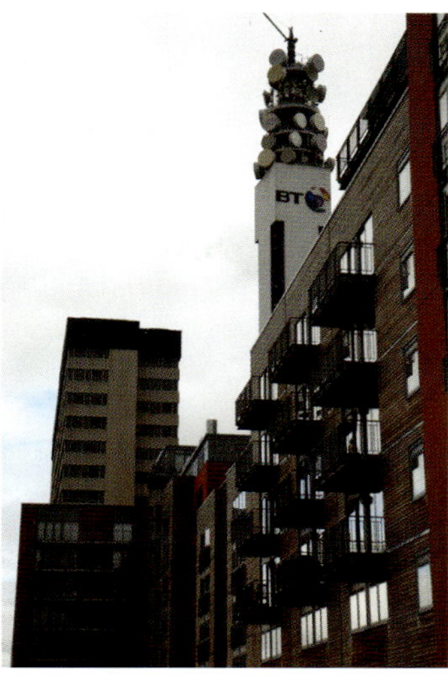

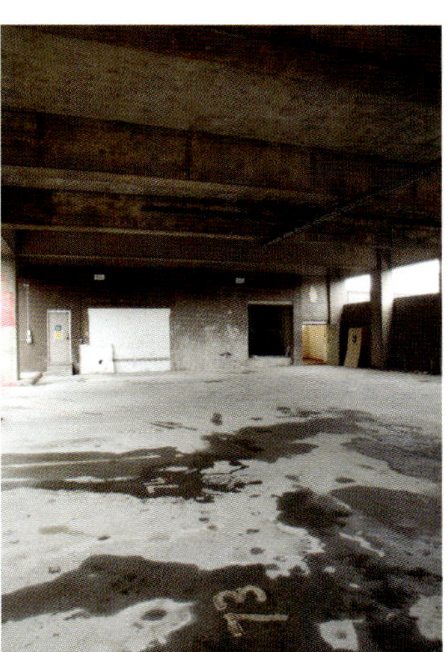

own local pubs and shops, have gradually run down; while former industrial areas, in the centre, have been rapidly transformed by a new vogue for apartment living. Levitating above the urban landscape, symbols of a new wave of economic regeneration, these upwardly mobile spaces appear to be exclusively targetted at professional single people. When you open the doors and go inside them, you understand the reason – there is barely any room for anyone else.

The installation version of Wearing's 'Family History' moves in, like an unexpected long-term house-guest, into two of these pristine 'show home' spaces. In the Forbury apartments in Reading, residents of this local bastion of luxury living have a panoramic view of all you could wish to see of the Berkshire metropolis, which, if you know where you're looking, takes in the street where 'The Family' was filmed. At Brindley House in Birmingham, the metamorphosis of one of the city's largest and most unsightly office blocks into a gleaming citadel of miniature condominiums is not yet complete. There is a makeshift sales entrance for potential buyers, though for Wearing's installation you go in the back way, up a graffitied stairwell, past exposed Seventies concrete, through the dusty remnants of an earlier era.

Inside the apartments where the installation is located, most of the furniture has been removed. Two virtually identical (and increasingly generic) living/dining rooms act as the setting for a large-scale video projection of the interview between Heather and Trisha; their makeover into magazine-cover interiors mirrored, in the projected image, by the soothing, similarly aspirational mise-en-scène of the television studio set. Next door, in the box-room bedroom, the only thing on display is a small LCD monitor, into which you peer, as if through a keyhole, at a very different domestic scene.

Prompting its own vivid flashback to the 1970s, this miniature looking-glass world is a facsimile reconstruction of the living room in the Wearings' former family home in Birmingham. As the sequence begins, a young girl, looking not unlike the ten-year-old Gillian, settles herself in front of the television set, on which the distinctive title sequence of 'The Family' (the camera dissolving down from a city skyline to a family living room to family portrait on top of a TV set) has started to play.

The illusion is so complete that these images of the stand-in Gillian appear almost to merge with the footage of 'The Family' – the act of spectatorship seemingly blurred by the childlike intensity of her identification. Although hanging on their every word, you can tell, as she turns to speak to the camera, that she hasn't always fully understood what she's seen and heard. As the brief cameo comes to a close, and you return to the conversation between Trisha and Heather, the image of the child watching and waiting stays in your head. It is a kind of archetypal family tableau: the adults talking together in the main room, the child listening in from a distance. From the child's grave expression, you can tell that she already knows that all the action in life is happening elsewhere: on the other side of the screen, or on the other side of a wall.

At the end of the piece, as a final coup de théâtre, the camera tracks back to reveal that both the living room and the television studio are each total fabrications, built side by side on a large sound stage. A symbol of how television brings us into increasingly intimate proximity with other people's lives, this Brechtian manoeuvre also hints at how the documentary ambitions of series like 'The Family' have been superseded by the newer and flashier offspring of celebrity culture and reality TV. It also can't fail but to draw

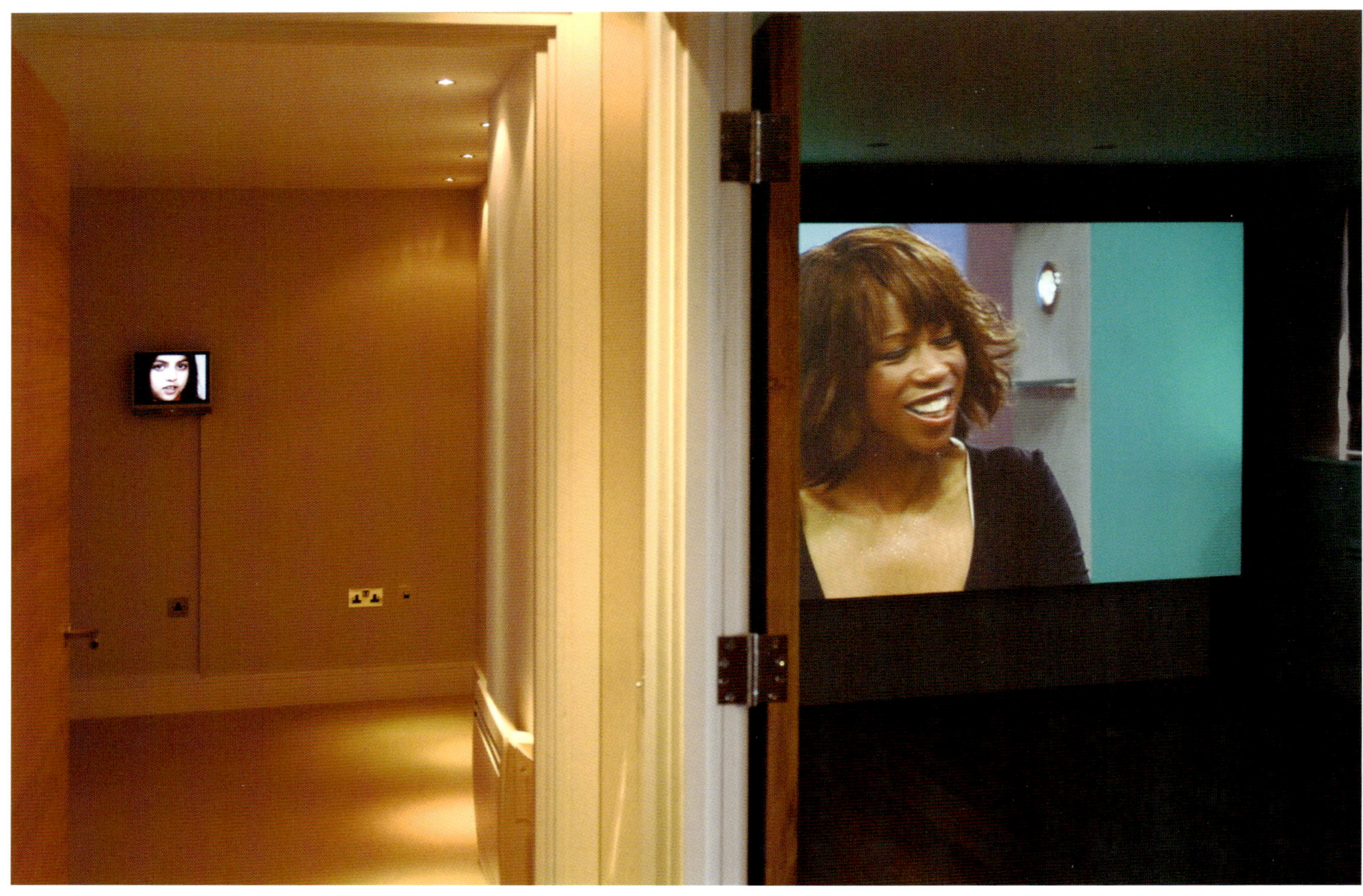

your attention to the artifice of the architectural space in which the installation is located; former offices, warehouses and factories that used to hum with the bustle of working people, turned into lifestyle palaces for a virtual demographic. Although it wears its cultural commentary lightly, 'Family History', in its reflection on the changes in British society and television over the last thirty years, homes in on one of the fundamental fault-lines that distinguishes the 1970s from the present day – in the social (and institutional) realm, so much of what used to be public has become private; while, in the individual (and emotional) realm, so much of what used to be private has become public.

While it engages with some of these wider themes, 'Family History' is, at its heart, a highly personal work – a portrait of one child of television by another; a woman who, to a significant extent, grew up on television rendered, affectionately and acutely, by an artist who grew up with television. Blending biography and auto-biography, it is a piece that uses the language of television, not in a spirit of appropriation or the service of reconstruction or deconstruction, but as a shared vernacular language with which both artist and subject are familiar; a language, indeed, with which we are all familiar; a language which, even more now than in the 1970s, is real to us – a language of the everyday.

STEVEN BODE

THAT TV FAMILY SPLITS UP

By ROGER BEAM

T V's most celebrated real-life family has broken up.

Outspoken Margaret Wilkins and her husband Terry are living apart. And the others have gone their separate ways.

The Wilkins became overnight stars three years ago in the BBC documentary series The Family.

Nine million viewers watched fascinated every Wednesday night as they lived the day-to-day life of an "ordinary household."

And as the cameras whirred. Terry pledged: "The family is **NOT** going to break up after this.

"Not like the American couple who went on T V like us and after it the husband and wife got divorced."

Now the Wilkins's 24-year marriage is on the rocks. Bus driver Terry lives alone in a bedsitter.

And 42-year-old Margaret said: "I don't think there's much hope of us getting back together again. We're two different personalities.

"I'm more outgoing and Terry is a quieter sort of person. We started quarrelling so it's for the best."

She added: "It's got nothing to do with the television programme."

Alone

In 1974 nine members of the Wilkins family and a four man TV crew crowded into Margaret's flat in Whitley Street, Reading. Berks.

Now she lives there alone with 12-year-old son Chris, her love child by another man.

Daughter Marian and husband Tom Bernes. whose marriage was a highlight in the series, have their own home—and a baby girl.

Son Gary and wife Karen have a council house and two small sons.

And independent 19-year-old Heather has set up home on her own.

Terry, 42, who had a heart operation last year, said: "Margaret and I are still good friends."

TOGETHERNESS: The Wilkins family as viewers saw them three years ago.

SC: You present a young actress playing yourself as a child in 'Family History'.
Given that so much of your work deals with television, and with notions of reality
and documentary, what are your memories of watching the show at that age? Does
the programme still weigh heavily in your thoughts?

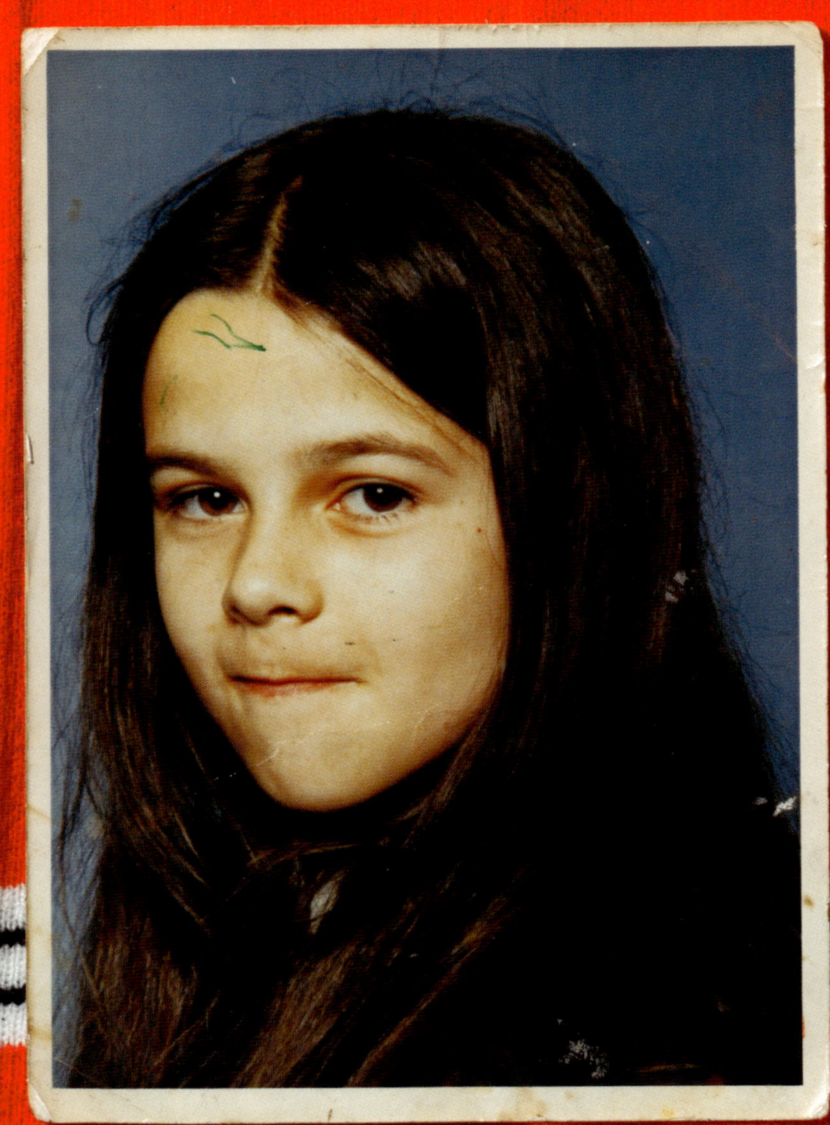

SCHOOL PHOTO OF ME AGED 10 1/2

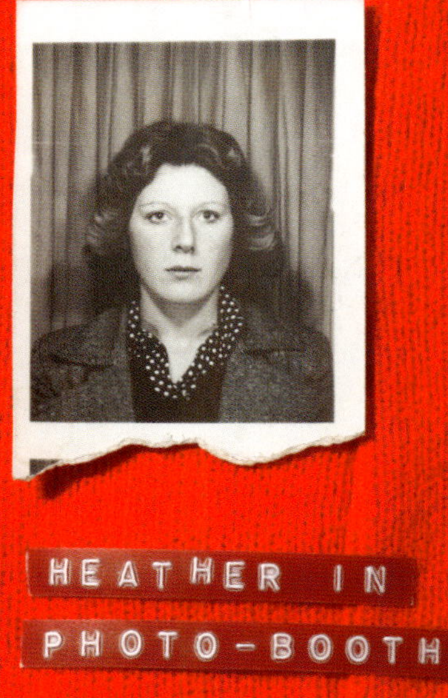

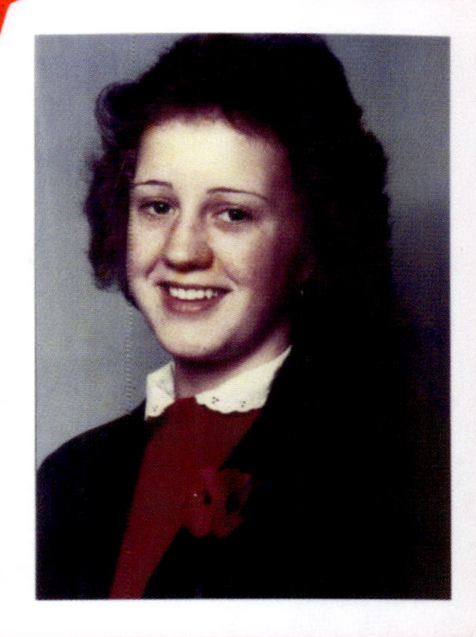

GW: I watched loads of television as a child —quite a lot of it on my own…But I do have a very clear memory of watching 'The Family' when I was around ten. It's a image that came back to me very forcefully around 1990, at a time when I had just left art school and was thinking of becoming a filmmaker and maybe even going to film school. I had borrowed a friend's Video 8 camera and was beginning doing vox pops in the street. It's strange…at the moment when I was using the vox pops to encourage these spontaneous reactions from people, I had my own personal flashback to 'The Family', almost like a kind of epiphany.

The great thing about 'The Family', for me, at any rate, was that there was no voiceover telling you what to think. It had the same unrehearsed quality that I was trying to get with my work. TV in Britain at the time wasn't very inspiring, and there were reports that documentary departments were being closed down because people had lost interest in the form. I hadn't seen 'The Family' for years but the programme, or at least the image of it that had stayed in my head, formed a real connection with what I was trying to achieve with my own work.

SC: Did you ever find yourself comparing your own family to the Wilkins family in the programme?

GW: I remember I related to Heather, the youngest daughter, even though she was a few years older than me. She was rebellious, and outspoken; she fought with her parents and with authority figures at her school. When you are that age, you always look up to someone slightly older than you, but I remember also that she reminded me of my friend Christine, who I used to think looked quite a lot like her. When I look at pictures of the two of them now, I can't really see the resemblance, so I think I must have joined the dots over the years in my imagination to make them seem as one.

GW: I can't remember ever getting bored in front of the TV! When I saw 'The Family' again, many years later, there were things in the programme of which I had absolutely no recollection, probably because they had made no great impression on me…But there was a lot that I remembered really vividly – the arguments and fights, in particular, all of which seemed to involve Heather…These would have been some of the main things that would have stood out, especially to a ten year old girl, but I can also remember a lot of other, more everyday stuff that, at times, felt a bit like a mirror of things that were going on in my own family.

SC: One of the remarkable things about 'The Family' and its predecessor, 'An American Family,' which was broadcast the previous year in the United States, is that private, domestic details were broadcast to such substantial audiences and made public on a mass scale for the first time. The camera entered one family's living room and, in doing so, created a cultural phenomenon that generated a major level of public conversation, making celebrities out of 'normal' people. By contrast, your early work as an artist is much more about anonymous people encountered in passing, such as the vox pops you've mentioned, which involve filming in public, on the street. Did you find that the camera helped you approach people? Did you find it intimidating at all to work that way?

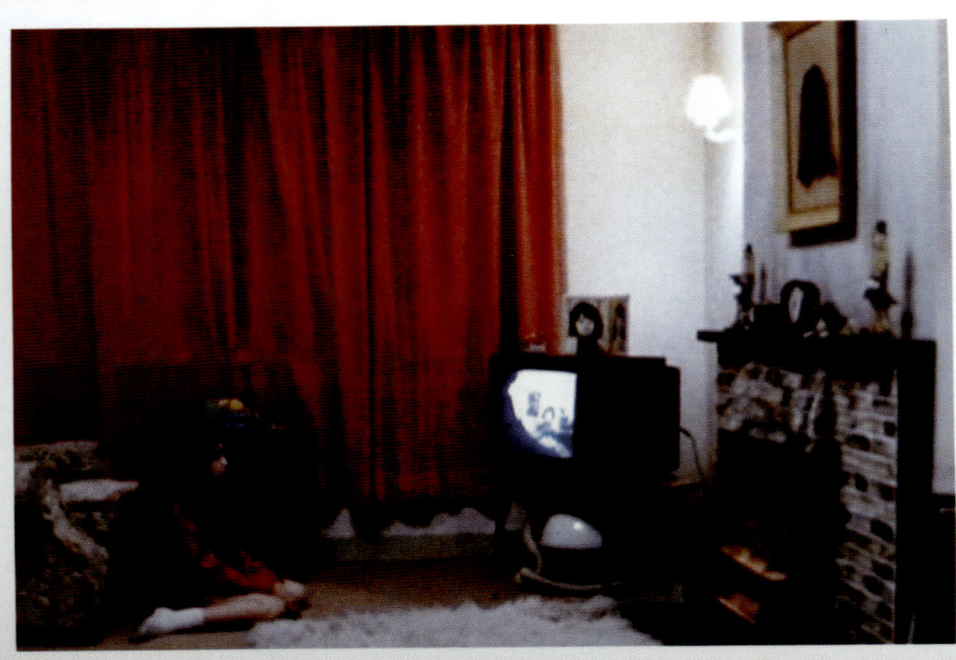

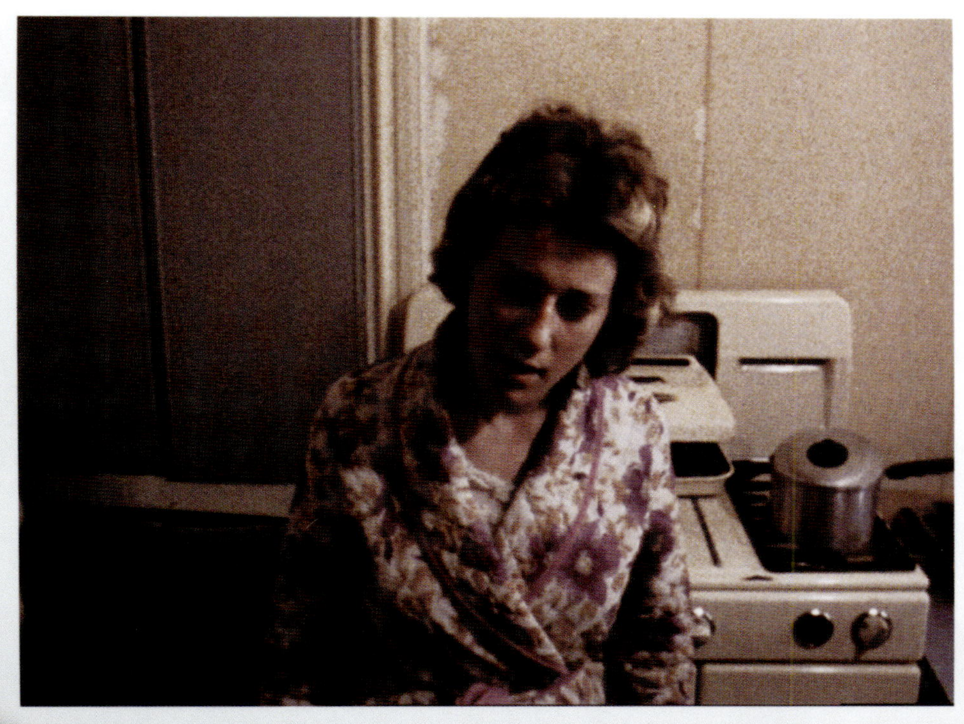

GW: I think you can almost see life more clearly through a camera than you can in reality. It forces you to make certain decisions; and makes you less inhibited about talking to people. Going back to the 1990s vox pops, I found it very exciting that they not only gave me an opportunity to reach out and talk to people, but that they also gave those people a vehicle to say things for which there might not be any other opportunity. At the time, documentaries still needed a very strong argument or 'message' to stand a chance of getting made, and that's why it's quite interesting going back to 'The Family,' it didn't. It simply presented a family – a very normal, banal subject – and showed that through everyday subject matter you could discover quite universal things about people.

SC: In the vox pops you got these quick takes, and that's it. In most cases you didn't have prolonged engagement with the subjects. Early reality television shows from the Seventies both in Britain and in the States were more durational. They came out of a verité tradition, exemplified by directors like Frederick Wiseman, and also have an interesting relationship to Andy Warhol's notions of duration and filming 'reality'. The programmes provided a long-term engagement with the families, there were characters developed whom viewers could begin to know somewhat intimately.

GW: There is something very immediate about the vox pop that sometimes gets you closer to the truth because people don't have time to adjust to the camera and prepare for the situation. Because of this, the relationship between the interviewer and the interviewee is more transparent. The observational documentary is more complex in that it <u>seems</u> completely transparent, but you don't know how much the director has set up a scene or provoked a situation, or how much the person being filmed is behaving especially for it.

'The Family' was made in fly-on-the-wall style but there were also moments when the family members were interviewed by Paul Watson. It was actually these interviews, more than any of the more observational sections, that brought out some of the more sensational aspects of their lives, like when Margaret confessed that her youngest son Christopher was the product of an affair. 'The Family' wasn't strictly, or wholly, an observational documentary; it used a combination of documentary, observation and interview to make it appeal to a mass audience, knowing that a regular series of revelations would keep people's interest.

'The Family' was on every week for three months, so people's original ideas about the Wilkins (which were often quite negative) would change as viewers became more familiar with them. As one viewer put it when she was interviewed about the programme: 'the family isn't that bad, really, when you get to know them'. I think this process of 'getting to know them' normalised some of the issues that were represented and reversed people's initial prejudices. In effect, you were getting to know a family in a not dissimilar way to how you get to know anyone, over time. There is a similarity also to soaps and TV mini-series, where characters grow on you over weeks or months. It took many years for this idea to be explored again with real people. In fact it wasn't until the early Nineties with MTV's 'The Real World' and the British docu-soaps of the mid-Nineties, and now 'Big Brother'. Critics of these programmes often tend to see only one episode and, of course, the programmes don't work at all if you only watch one, because there is no narrative and you are normally left feeling indifferent to everyone. It is only by watching numerous episodes that you can properly make sense of people's actions.

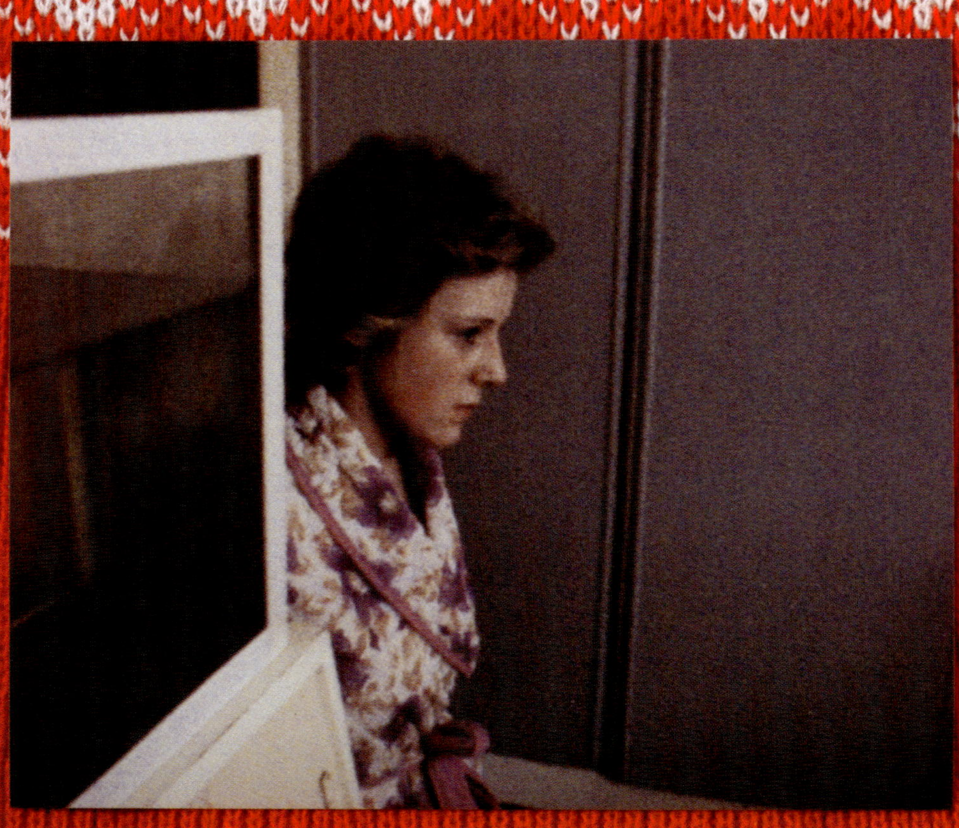

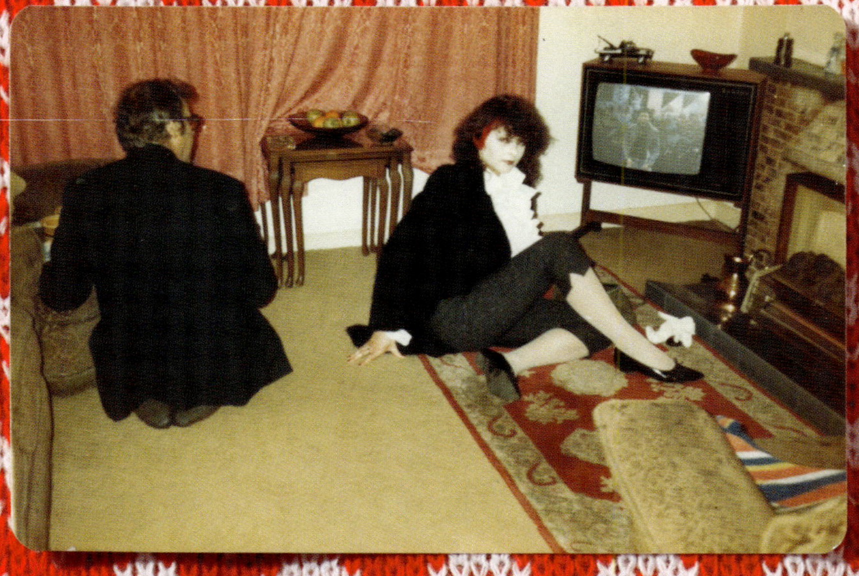

SC: In 'Family History' you revisit both 'The Family' and the actual moment and place in which you first experienced it: your childhood living room during the 1970s. After 'An American Family' was broadcast there were subsequent documentaries made about the family that revisited the series and gauged what had happened to the Loud family since the original broadcast. In 'Family History', you construct a situation in which histories of both you as a viewer and Heather as one of the subjects of 'The Family' are implicated.

GW: Yes. I wanted to show how my past includes the memory of being a passive observer of someone else's life. I wanted the past and present to sit next door to each other as if you could literally walk from the present into the past. In my head those things sit alongside each other, and that's what I wanted to show. I was also interested in the whole process of revisiting the subjects themselves, which, as you mention, is something that television has already done anyway. In the same way that there was a follow-up programme on the Loud family, there was also one on the Wilkins family, around ten years after the series first aired. I especially wanted to focus on Heather, who for me was always the main character in 'The Family', and get a sense of her life and her thoughts thirty-two years on. I knew that didn't want to revisit her in her current home environment, so I had the idea of interviewing her in a kind of chat-show setting. Chat shows are increasingly based around this stylised approximation of a living room, in which people feel so 'at home' that they will reveal things about themselves…

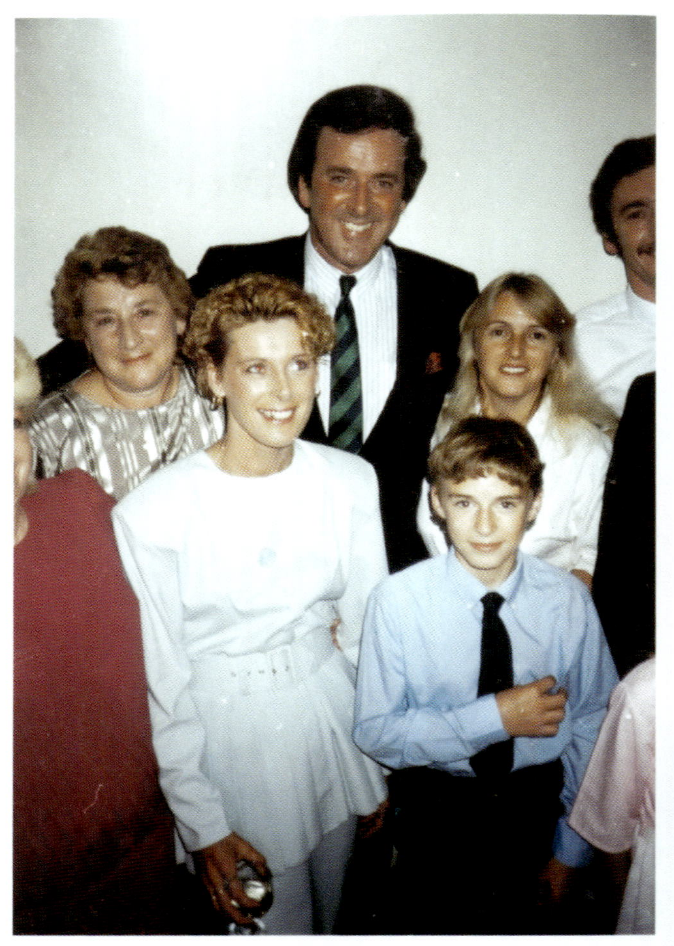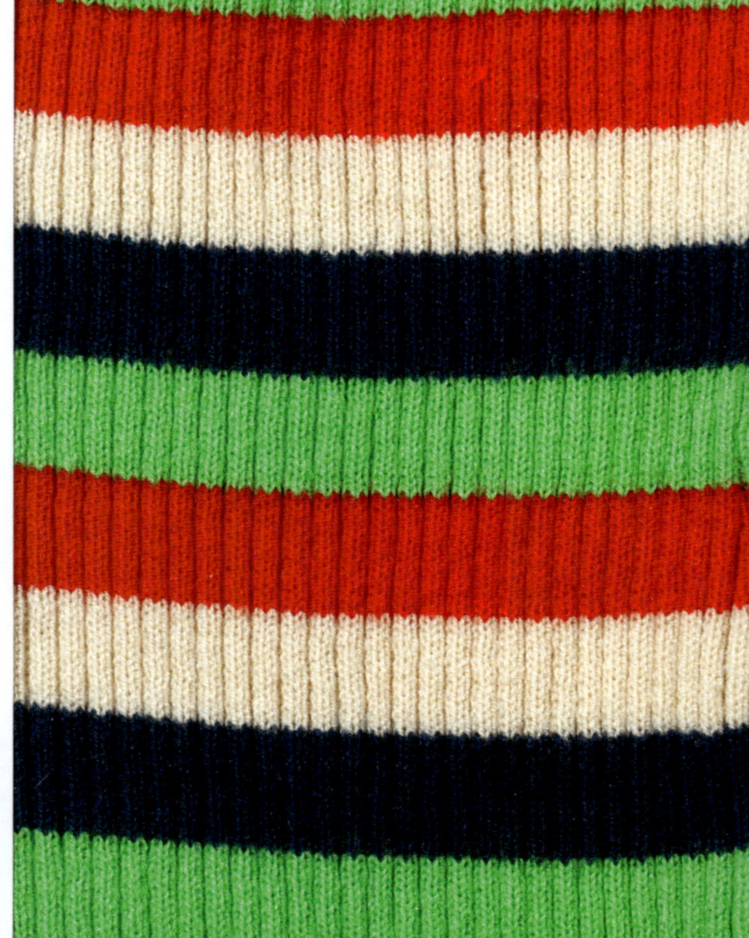

THE WILKINS FAMILY
WITH TERRY WOGAN

SC: Exactly, it's about trying to create the illusion that you've entered into somebody else's private space somehow…

GW: But at the same time, it's a false intimacy. The interview may come across as spontaneous, but it's likely that the person interviewed will either have anticipated or had some knowledge of the questions and worked out their answers in advance. In researching this project, I became very interested in the mechanics of daytime chat shows, and how they have an incredibly finely-tuned, orchestrated way of drawing people into a conversation. It was only from looking closely at these shows that I became fully aware of all the numerous cameras that are used for even the most simple interview: the head shot, the three-quarters body shot, the various crane cameras or cameras on a track. When edited together, they have an almost comforting, choreographed feeling…It's something that's easily taken for granted but I think it's a clever way to keep you glued to the programme so you never become bored.

SC: You've mentioned that in the early Nineties documentaries were falling out of favour, but recently Michael Moore has heralded the advent of the 'mega documentary,' and suddenly documentaries are big business, coinciding with the popularity of 'Big Brother' and other kinds of reality programming. 'Family History' scrambles all of these formats, as well as other television genres such as the game show and, as you've just mentioned, the chat show. There are multiple sets and multiple players juxtaposed against one another, which drives home this question about what actually constitutes the 'real' when everything is staged to a certain extent. It's something you've dealt with in your previous work, but I think this new project indicates the complex processes by which these structures increasingly feed into one another. How did you prepare Heather to participate in this project?

GW: I really only had a couple of meetings with her because I didn't want it to be too rehearsed. I also think she's very savvy, in that she's obviously very conscious of the mechanics of television, and quite aware of how to perform. I also suspect she has played with the idea of who she was then and who she is now many times. I don't think it was easy for her, as 'The Family' was made during one of the most sensitive periods of her life and a lot of things that would normally have remained personal and private were filmed for everyone to see. People had her down as volatile teenager who was being written off as a 'no hoper'. There's a scene in 'The Family' in which the careers adviser brushes Heather aside as if there was no future for her. The editing reinforces this point of view by cutting to the father driving a bus, the brother being a conductor, and the mum waiting outside her grocery store. It was probably the most pointed editing in the whole series, and again ran counter to the more observational method of filming by having a very particular point to make.

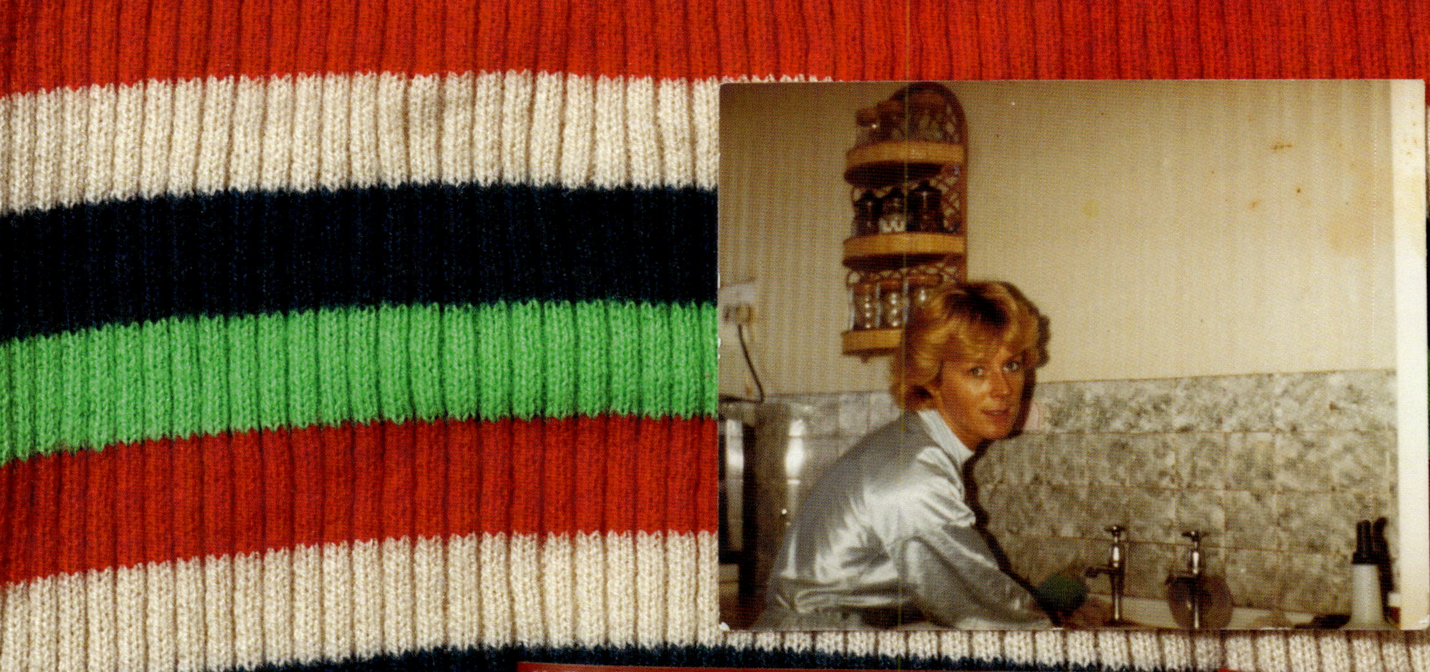

SC: Alan and Susan Raymond, the husband and wife team who were the cameramen for 'An American Family', really became part of the Loud family during shooting, they became close friends. It allowed them much more access to the situation, and everybody eventually felt quite comfortable with one another. But then the footage was wrested away from the Raymonds and given to a team of editors who were working with the producer, Craig Gilbert, who had a very specific idea in mind of what he wanted to happen. The family felt totally betrayed by the way it was edited, or more specifically to the way audiences reacted to the edit. It's not just the fact that they saw themselves on camera, but that the editing process manipulated the story to such an extent.

GW: When people are being filmed they always underestimate the extent to which editing can influence the way they are perceived. 'Big Brother' contestants usually complain that it is not their behaviour in front of the camera that has got them evicted, but how the editing has made them look. Programmes like 'Big Brother' or 'Celebrity Love Island' have gone to extreme lengths to make 'real life' into entertainment, that when you look back at 'The Family' it all seems so innocent in comparison.

What reality shows often do with people is keep them frozen in time. 'The Family' only ever captured a very short period of the Wilkins family's life, but because it was played out in front of so many millions of people it is the image that has stuck, or the one they have been stuck with. I think this is what drove Heather on in her career and her life —the Heather of today has fought so hard against her initial image, that I see her as quite a different person now. She knew she had to prove her critics wrong; her story in a way is a triumph over her TV image.

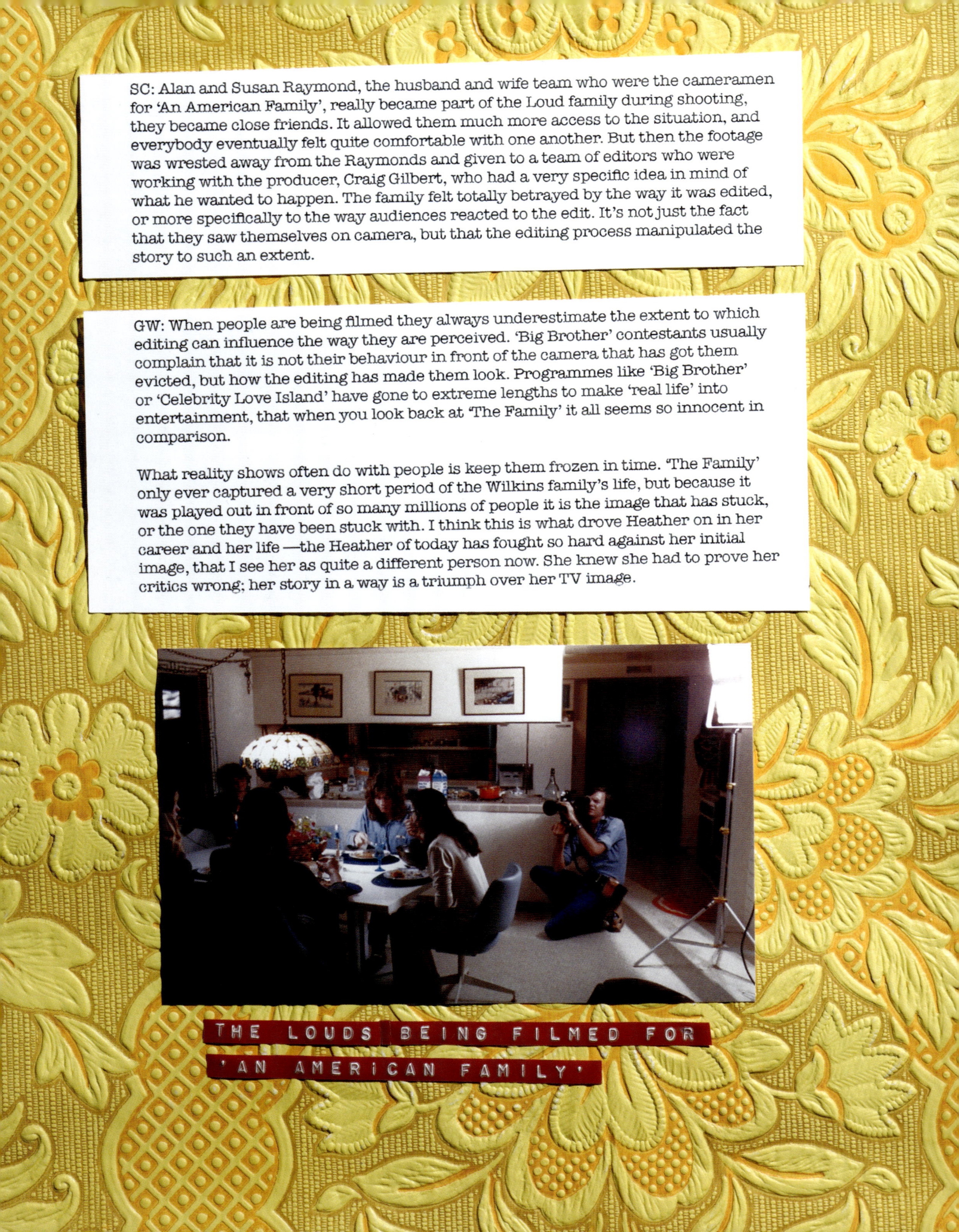

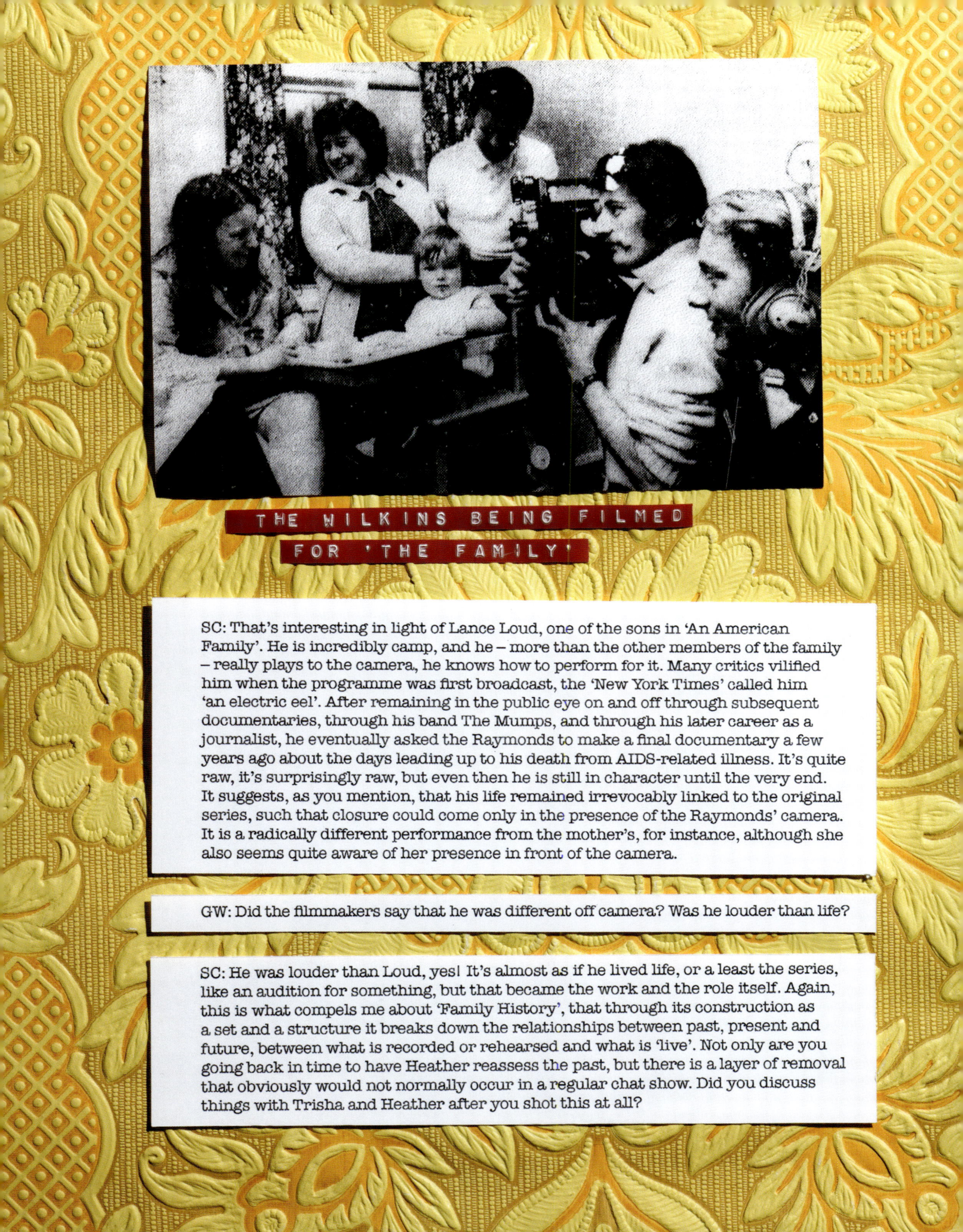

SC: That's interesting in light of Lance Loud, one of the sons in 'An American Family'. He is incredibly camp, and he – more than the other members of the family – really plays to the camera, he knows how to perform for it. Many critics vilified him when the programme was first broadcast, the 'New York Times' called him 'an electric eel'. After remaining in the public eye on and off through subsequent documentaries, through his band The Mumps, and through his later career as a journalist, he eventually asked the Raymonds to make a final documentary a few years ago about the days leading up to his death from AIDS-related illness. It's quite raw, it's surprisingly raw, but even then he is still in character until the very end. It suggests, as you mention, that his life remained irrevocably linked to the original series, such that closure could come only in the presence of the Raymonds' camera. It is a radically different performance from the mother's, for instance, although she also seems quite aware of her presence in front of the camera.

GW: Did the filmmakers say that he was different off camera? Was he louder than life?

SC: He was louder than Loud, yes! It's almost as if he lived life, or a least the series, like an audition for something, but that became the work and the role itself. Again, this is what compels me about 'Family History', that through its construction as a set and a structure it breaks down the relationships between past, present and future, between what is recorded or rehearsed and what is 'live'. Not only are you going back in time to have Heather reassess the past, but there is a layer of removal that obviously would not normally occur in a regular chat show. Did you discuss things with Trisha and Heather after you shot this at all?

GW: No, we discussed things with Trisha beforehand, and we suggested that she should start with the history of 'The Family' and then move into the present.

SC: Did she remember the programme from her own childhood?

GW: Yes, her father was a psychologist and she recalled that there was a spin-off programme in which psychologists talked about 'The Family'. She remembered that the psychologists' view was very old-fashioned. They were looking down on the working classes and even made a comment to the effect that the working classes are normally 'non-verbal' and that Paul Watson had made them more verbal somehow. Anyway, we had a meeting in which Trisha viewed the tapes and then set up some questions. She wanted the whole thing to be as spontaneous as possible.

SC: You have done projects for television in the past. Although 'Family History' isn't actually for broadcast on television, it uses and is about television. The history of video art goes hand in hand with that of broadcast television; do you think there's an interesting relationship between art and television at the moment? Where do you think it might be going?

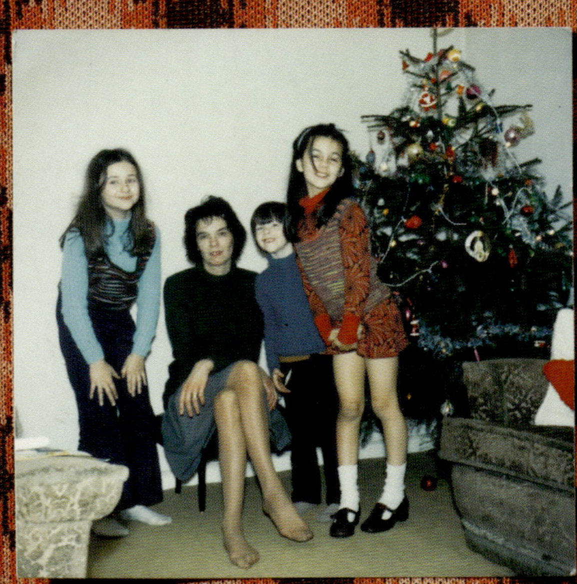

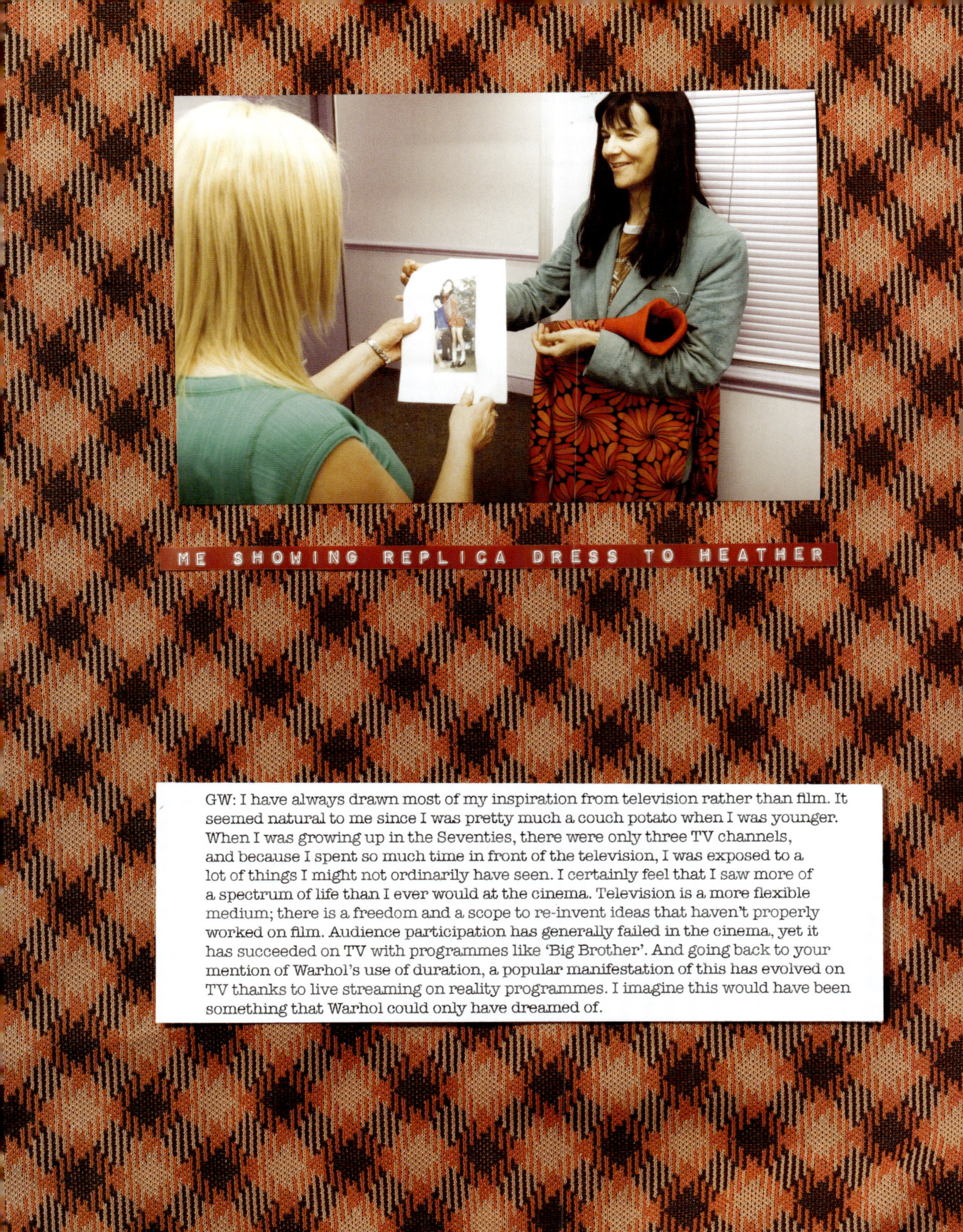

GW: I have always drawn most of my inspiration from television rather than film. It seemed natural to me since I was pretty much a couch potato when I was younger. When I was growing up in the Seventies, there were only three TV channels, and because I spent so much time in front of the television, I was exposed to a lot of things I might not ordinarily have seen. I certainly feel that I saw more of a spectrum of life than I ever would at the cinema. Television is a more flexible medium; there is a freedom and a scope to re-invent ideas that haven't properly worked on film. Audience participation has generally failed in the cinema, yet it has succeeded on TV with programmes like 'Big Brother'. And going back to your mention of Warhol's use of duration, a popular manifestation of this has evolved on TV thanks to live streaming on reality programmes. I imagine this would have been something that Warhol could only have dreamed of.

Both video art and reality television go back to the idea of portable cameras becoming more widely available and people having the opportunity to film themselves and record even the most trivial and unlikely aspects of their lives. We now have the website YouTube, where almost anything anyone has filmed can be uploaded and fulfil a desire for a potential audience. We live in a world where huge numbers of people want to be watched and appreciated, rather than disappear and become invisible.

SC: In the early days of video, artists like Vito Acconci and Joan Jonas were using the most advanced equipment in their studios and they were also turning the camera on themselves. We seem to have a compulsive habit to represent ourselves. The more advanced we become technically; the more we zoom in for the most intimate material. The action of making the private sphere public is becoming increasingly interesting and complex. Do you know, actually, how the Wilkins family was cast?

GW: There were advertisements put out. The producers may well have chosen Reading because it's seen as a kind of typical, average town. It's where a lot of MORI opinion polls are done, for example. I believe the Wilkins were chosen from around 100 candidates. Paul Watson did many interviews, and I think he realised during the first meeting with the Wilkins that they were 'it'. He had an intuitive feeling that they would make great television.

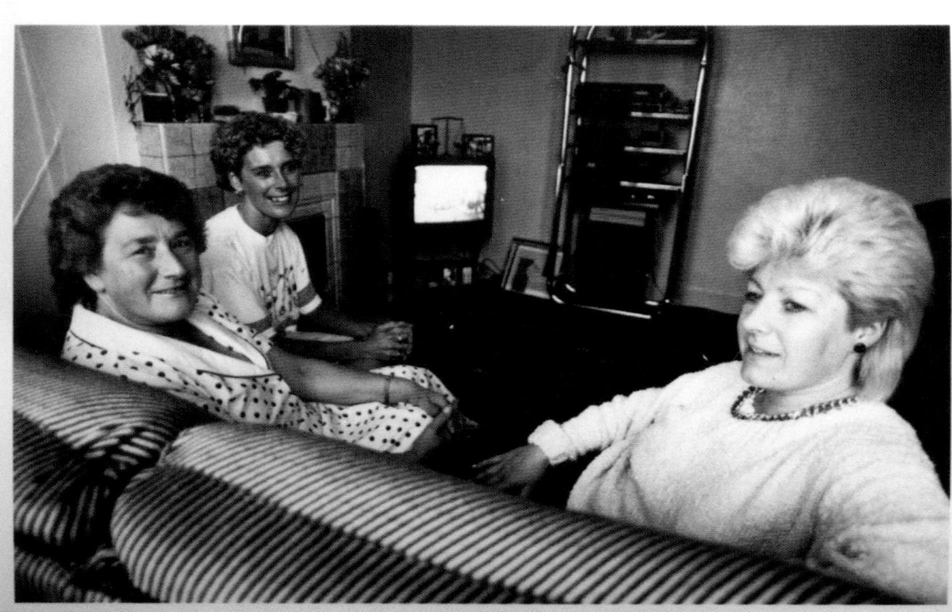

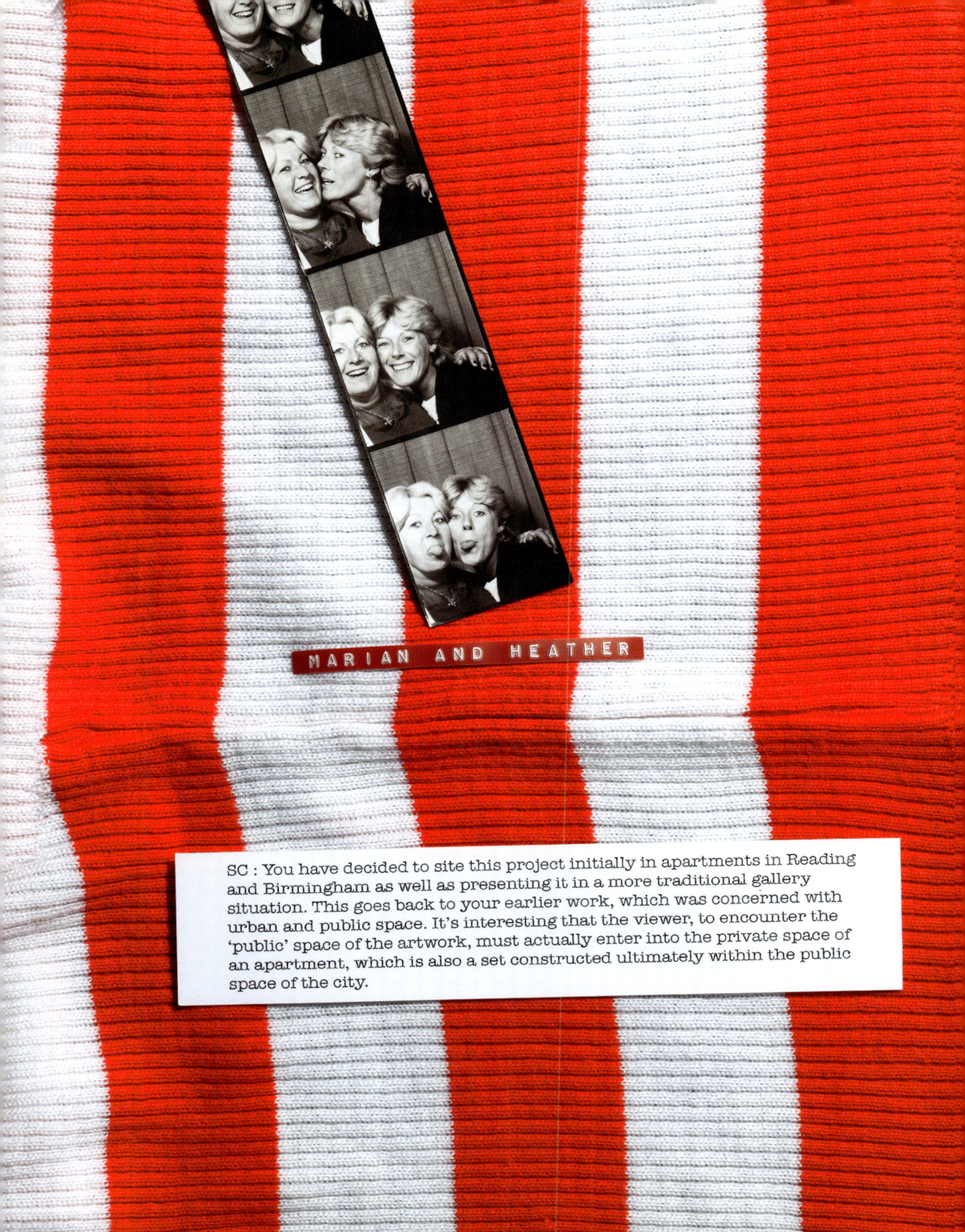

SC : You have decided to site this project initially in apartments in Reading and Birmingham as well as presenting it in a more traditional gallery situation. This goes back to your earlier work, which was concerned with urban and public space. It's interesting that the viewer, to encounter the 'public' space of the artwork, must actually enter into the private space of an apartment, which is also a set constructed ultimately within the public space of the city.

GW: Yes, that was the initial way of showing the piece, though it's worked well in a gallery setting too. I liked the installation in Birmingham, where a 'show flat' had been constructed in a disused office building that was in the process of being converted into apartments. You walked through this spacious building that had an almost 'warehouse gallery' feel to it until you reached these two small flats, impeccably made but totally incongruous to the space. It felt a bit like the property developers had had a hand in making their own kind of quasi-installation...

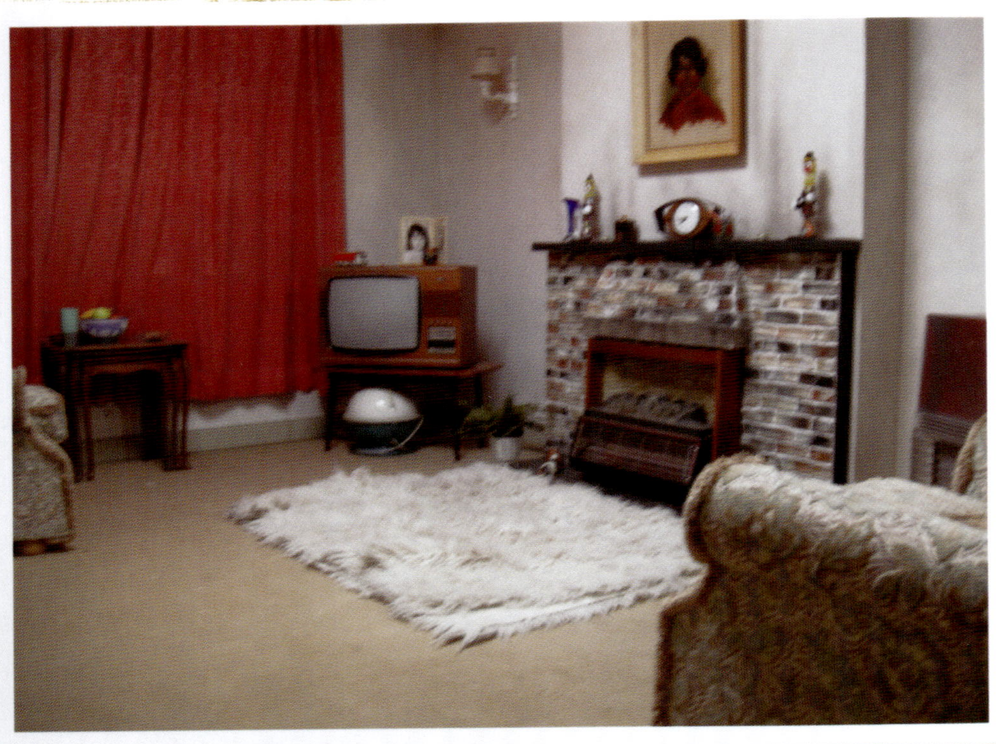

The purpose of showing the project in these show flats was to highlight changes in people's ideas and aspirations. In the Seventies, everyone's dream was to have a family house. This is no longer the overriding dream; there are now many more single people and a bigger emphasis on mobility. A flexible live/work space in an urban location is often more desirable, and it's interesting that the look of these spaces is echoed in the way that a lot of chat shows construct their sets. I did some research into Richard and Judy's show and looked at the construction of it. I discovered that all the props, like the tables and chairs, were sourced from places where the average viewer could have purchased them, the main outlet being IKEA. There is almost no difference now between what you see in people's living rooms and what you see in a TV studio!

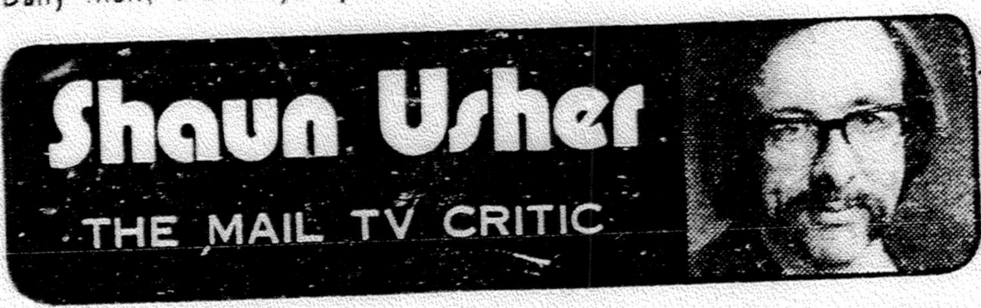

Imagine <u>your</u> family with these problems!

PAUL WATSON, the producer, never claimed that *The Family* (BBC 1) were typical, simply 'suitable.'

In other words, as ultimate electronic goldfish, the Wilkins clan is either honest and open, or totally lacking, in self-respect, according to one's upbringing and outlook.

Mrs Wilkins declared that the series, following her family from sunrise to sunset and beyond, would improve on what she called 'kitchen-sink drama,' by showing the real life of some ordinary people.

Sulking and science

She's right, in a cockeyed way, since no playwright would dare to burden an imaginary husband and wife with so many problems. The Wilkins have a genius, already well-defined although the programme has been running less than a month, for doing things the hard way.

One child is illegitimate, another cohabits with the lodger, the third had to get married. Last night's peepshow, concentrating on 15-year-old daughter Heather, disclosed that her boyfriend is a half-caste.

('To me, colour prejudice is ignorance,' said his white mother, while admitting that she'd never really taken to Pakistanis.)

Heather, who wants to be a hairdresser, but is being forced to spend an extra year at school, was discovered sulking through domestic science lessons.

She indulged in much defiance for its own sake, conducted with hanging boredom, which made it even more irritating, and compelled admiration for the teacher who nagged mildly instead of crowning the lady with her own grudgingly-prepared cake mixture.

But then came an interview with the Careers Officer, giving a hint of what frustrates working-class kids of all mental shades and sizes when they sense firm, unheeding pressure towards identical round holes.

Hairdressing, you remember, is Heather's vocation. 'Perhaps you haven't heard about opportunities in the catering trade,' the employment expert suggested, following up with a plug for the joys of Service life.

My uneasiness over this project, wiped out by the sheer revelatory drive of its opening chapter, has started to return.

The Wilkins don't have much of a life, but they are human. By bringing out the comedy of their situation (in my case, striking a nerve of snobbish horror, as well), the programme does tend to dwindle them into figures on a stage.

But I will be watching next week. The BBC may be doing wrong: if so, I am an unwilling, yet addicted accessory.

The price of heroics

The World at War (ITV) makes a chastening documentary contrast.

The latest edition, on America's Pacific battles, showed the true price of Hollywood Marine Corps heroics, with newsreel film of carnage as unrelentingly explicit as anyone can recall.

All in the cause of preserving civilisation as we know it — including the Wilkins family's freedom to wash its dirty linen in public, sponsored by the BBC and encouraged by people like me.

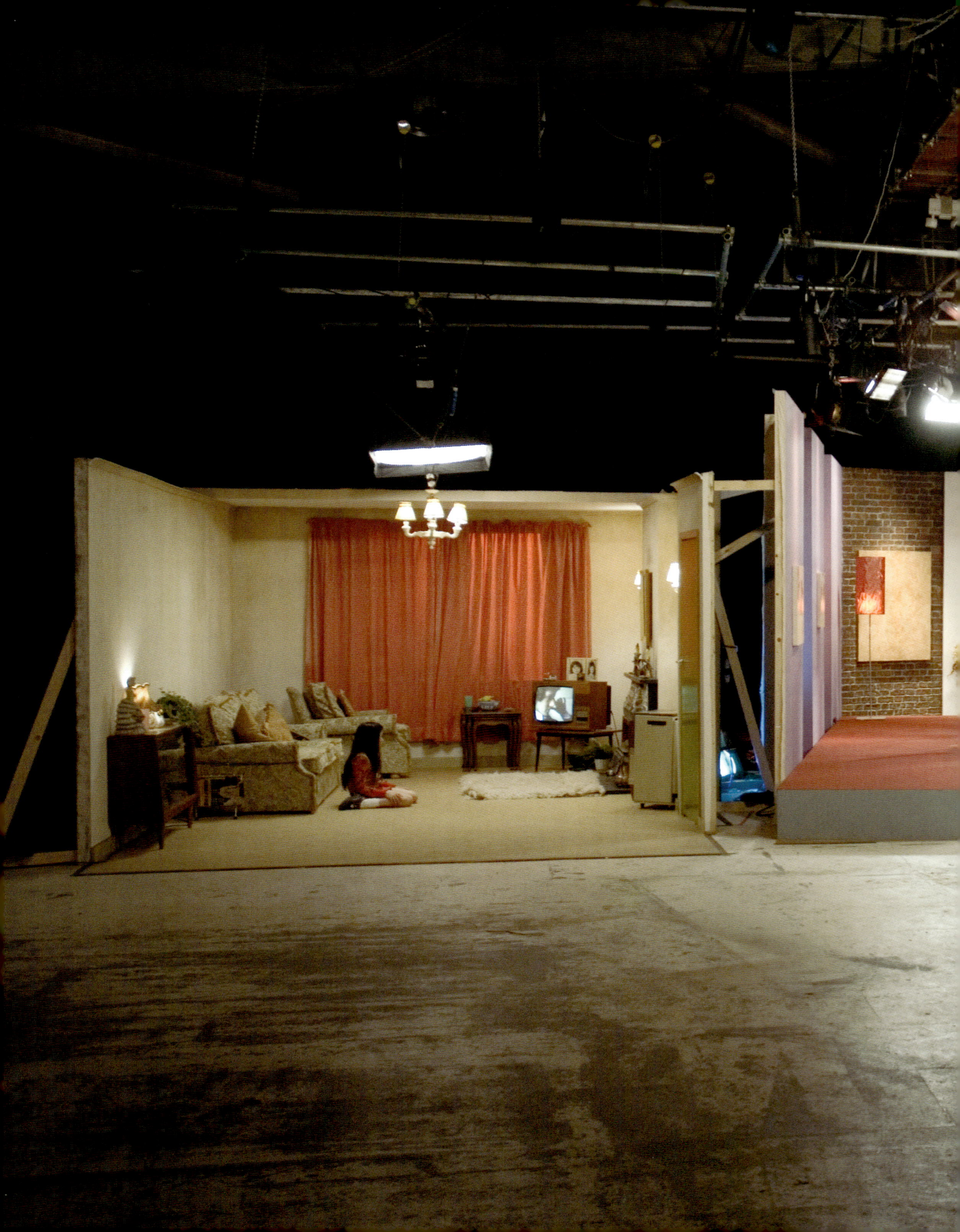

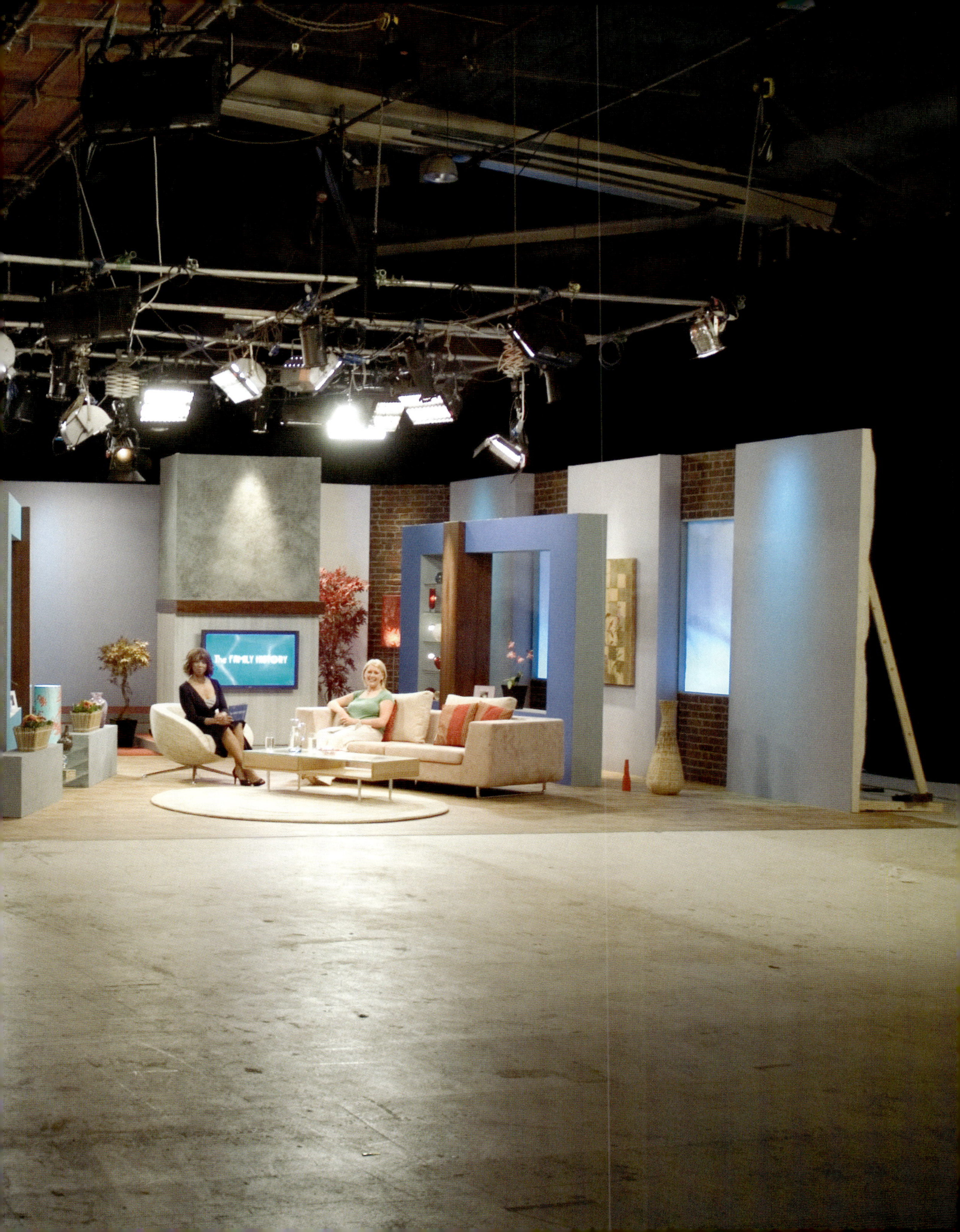
The FAMILY HISTORY

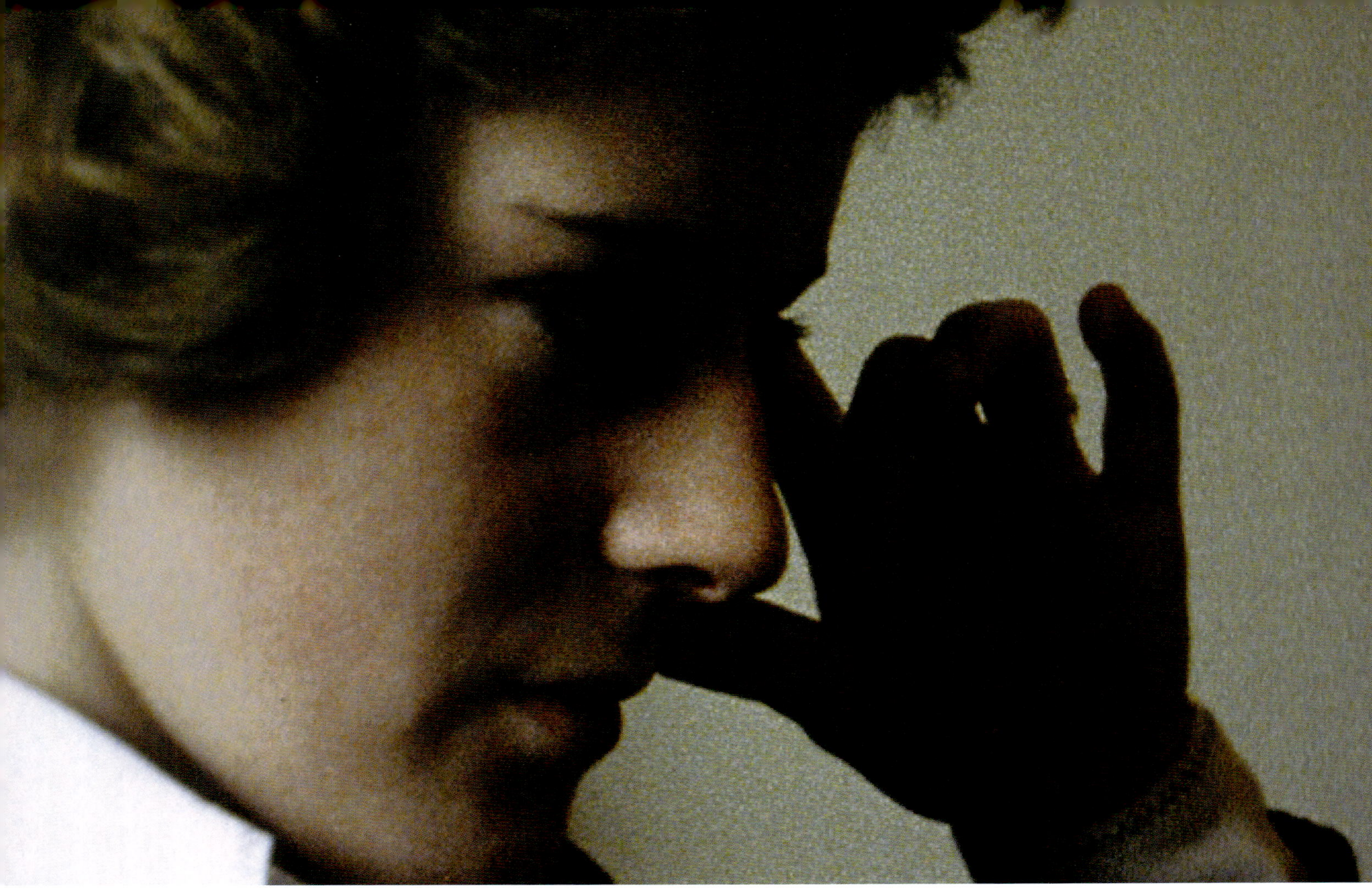

• 'The Family' (1974)

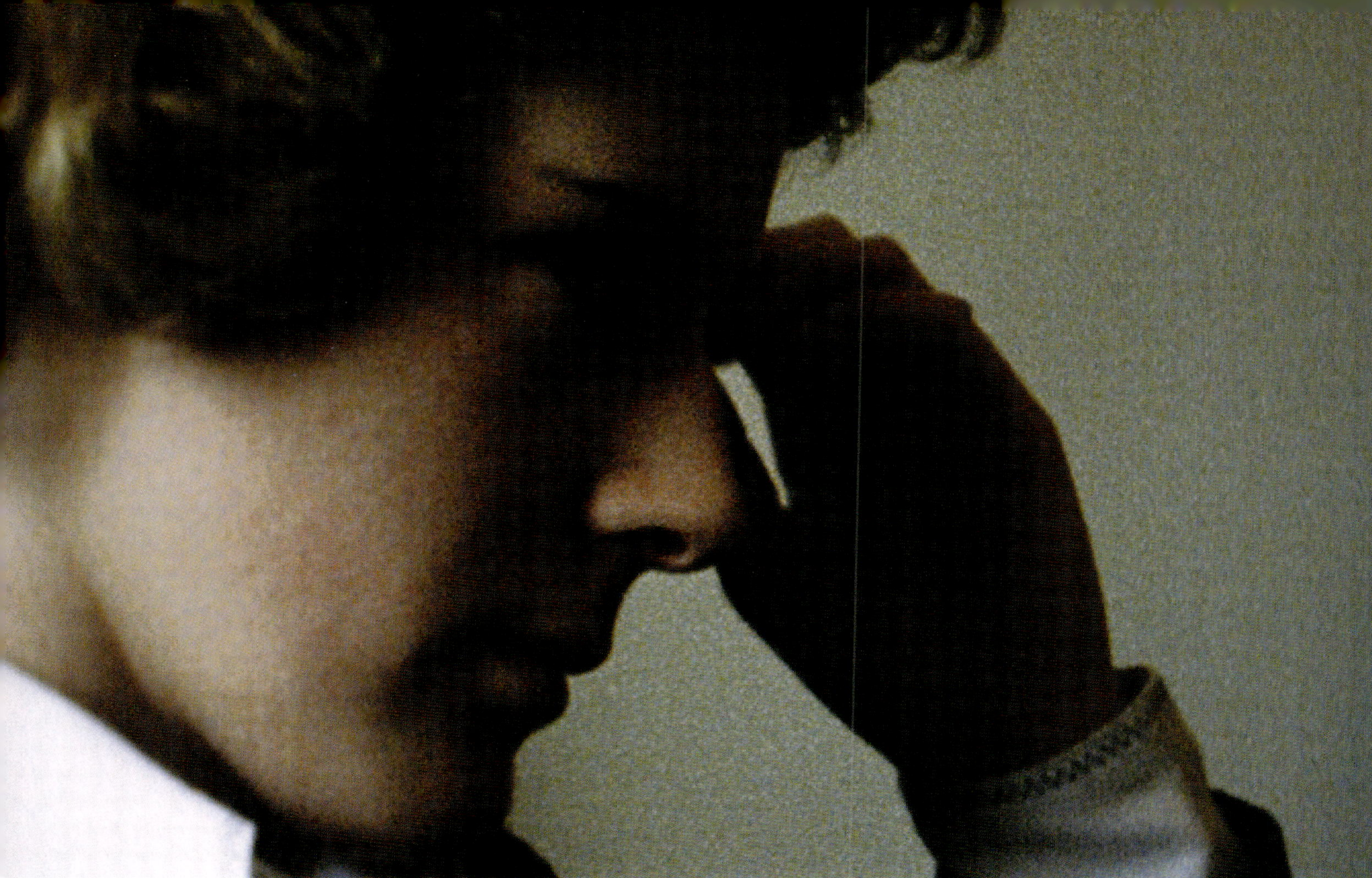

Careers Advisor:
Hello. It's Heather, is it?

Heather:
Yeah.

Careers Advisor:
Come sit down, Heather. As you know, I am the Careers officer and I've come here to have a general chat with you, really about your plans for the future and what you are hoping to do with yourself.
Well um… Well now Heather, tell me… I see you filled in a form a little while ago. I see that you do a hairdressing job on Saturdays. How long have you being doing this?

Heather:
Quite a while.

Careers Advisor:
Only I feel that you know you ought to be aware of other opportunities. Perhaps you haven't heard very much about opportunities in the catering trade. You see I'm… What I want to do is to tell you about other opportunities and make sure you have thought about all possible opportunities and also to tell you a little bit how employers feel if you're going to look for a job. An employer really is most interested in what kind of qualifications or what kind of educational standard you've reached and I was just wondering why you are so keen to leave school at Easter time when within six weeks or so you will be taking CSE's then. If any chance comes that you want to change your mind later on then you've still got something you can present to an employer to say you have qualified in such and such a subject, which you know you might regret later on. Have you not thought about this very much?

Heather:
I've thought about it but I didn't want to do it.

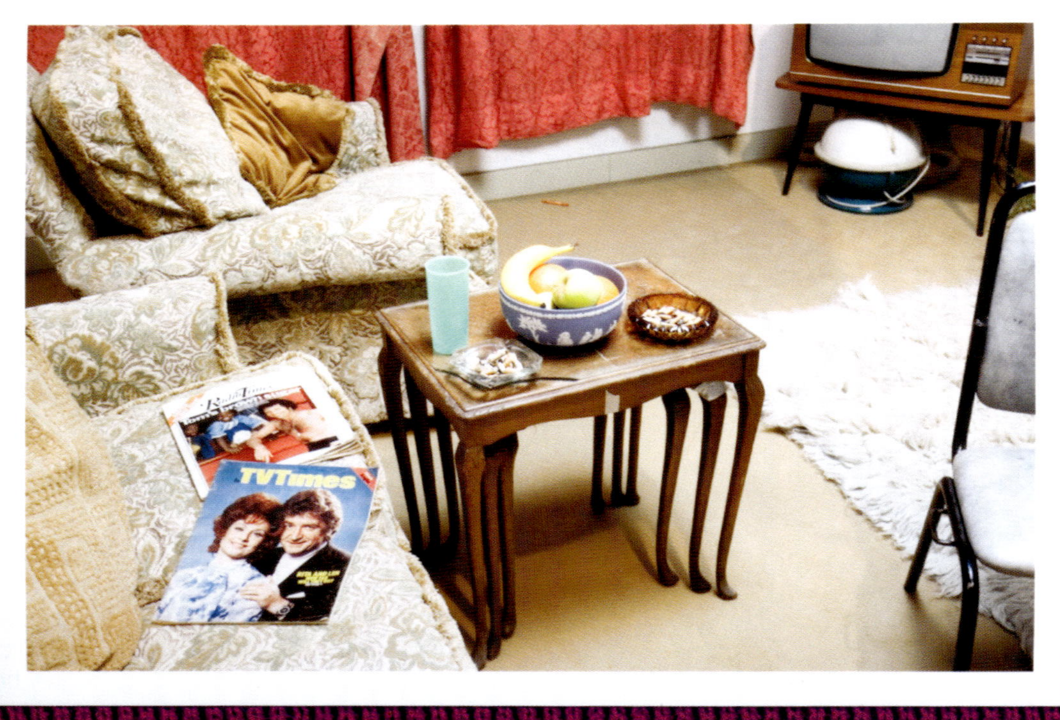

It's not often that you can find yourself in a room with Germaine Greer, Alice Cooper, Jade Goody, Neil Hamilton, Trisha Goddard, two members of Girls Aloud and a Spice Girl a little on the slight side with hair no longer the colour of ginger, Kate Lawler, Norman Mailer, Katie Price, Samuel Preston, Ruth Badger, Nick Bateman, Darren Gough, Anthea Turner, JG Ballard, a husband and wife pair who once cheated on 'Who Wants To Be A Millionaire', Chico, Jimmy Tarbuck, Jennie Bond, Carol Thatcher, Lord Brockett, Handy Andy, Jodie Marsh, Jean Baudrillard, Gillian Wearing, Jeremy Spake, Linda Barker, Ann Widdecombe, Les Dennis, Chantelle, Phil Tufnell, Myleene Klass, Maggot, Johnny Rotten, Janet Street Porter, Vanessa Feltz, the ghost of John Lennon and Sharon Osbourne's dog. We were like a family gathered together for a wedding, or a funeral. We were there to witness the joining together of Jordan and Peter Andre. We were there to witness the final falling out between Pete the Tourettes guy and Crazy Nikki. We were there to mourn the loss of the lead singer of Freddie and the Dreamers.

"We love to follow a story, to see how it ends. Once the story has started, however stupid or sordid the story might be, however lightweight, we find it hard not to follow it to its end. We have to watch. The attraction is not just in what you see, but in what might happen."

You get the feeling as the small talk in this room ebbs and slows, as Jade Goody chats with novelist about aroma and agents, as daughter of Iron Lady admires a Girl Aloud's tan, as tension between girls with experimentally proportioned teeth and chests is reduced by iconic feminist and slightly tipsy interior decorator, as Turner Prize winning artist discusses hype and light bulbs with The Cheeky Girls, that we are being watched. We are being filmed, and more crucially, we are being edited, turned into caricatures of ourselves, easily understood stereotypes, by shadowy figures in the middle distance.

"Reality television is just as compelling as any soap. Reality television is an intense game show where the contestants are encouraged to put their whole lives and futures on the line. Reality television is like finally managing to find out what your neighbours actually do behind closed doors. Reality TV is finding out that celebrities are genuinely better than we are and worthy of our respect for living such heroic lives/are actually useless idiots with no redeeming qualities that we can comfortably feel superior to. Reality TV suggests we like to be told what to do. Reality TV is a cynically co-ordinated hybrid of game show, talk show, soap, sports competition, sit-com, court of law, school playground and audition. Reality television is the voice of the masses under siege from an intellectual, commercial and political elite who don't want to relinquish power. Reality television reflects in parts the prevailing values of the society it inhabits – leisure, gambling, nosiness, voyeurism, cruelty, consumerism, fear of the unknown."

The punk legend eats a rat. The ex newspaper editor bares his chest. A girl proud to be known as a professional bitch throws up all over a disc jockey who came last in a singing competition broadcast by the BBC as if it was a contribution to the social health of the nation. The comedian has a nervous breakdown on pages 3, 5, 6, 7 and 8. The girl who came second in a modelling competition screened over twelve weeks on Living TV talks to Alan Whicker about her new travel series on Sky. The ex 'Big Brother' contestant who once got so drunk on live television that she stripped naked in an act that was part Francis Bacon, part 'Readers' Wives', part 'Carry On' and part Andy Warhol is politely explaining that her next projects include launching a perfume, writing a novel, making her West End debut and taking part in a celebrity golf tournament hosted by Ant and Dec. The cricketing dancer, or dancing cricketer, is fingering his groin, purely medicinally, in the presence of a soap actress who goes out with a member of Blue who once dated a girl who came third in a competition to find someone who could work as an assistant to a television chef who once ate a live lamb live on Channel 5 whilst answering questions on his specialist subject, the life and art of David Hockney.

"It's a constant fight between what viewers want to know about the participants and what the participants allow to be known about them."

In early 1974, when I was sixteen, I lived in a drab semi-detached house in Stockport. Life still seemed post war, rationed and reined in. Colour was a distant dream. The future didn't stretch much further than tomorrow. My hair was long and stringy.

I wore flared jeans and denim shirts and shoes with a flavour of a platform. I loved T.Rex, David Bowie and Roxy Music, but also, because I was a bit strange and lonely around the edges, Can, Henry Cow and Robert Wyatt. I lived with my mother, who was thirty six, my father, who was thirty seven, and my two younger sisters, aged thirteen and eight. I sometimes think this is all I ever really knew about them, apart from their names. We didn't do much as a family, and seemed to pass through the house like ghosts, connected by blood, location and time, but little else.

The one thing we did together was watch television. We watched 'Star Trek' and 'Coronation Street'. We watched 'Top of the Pops' and 'The Generation Game'. The whole nation appeared to be doing the same, stopping at the same time to laugh at Morecambe and Wise. Me and my Dad would watch 'Grandstand' and 'Match of the Day'. We ate Weetabix spread with marmalade. Our lettuce was coated with salad cream. We took three sugars in our tea. Soup was tinned and the sliced ham was transparent.

We did not appear on television and it never occurred to any of us that we ever would. We never talked to each other about the events inside this house that would lead within a few years to my father committing suicide. We just followed our fate, drawn towards a terrible end as if we knew all along, even as we laughed at Morecambe and Wise, that the conclusion to this family life was to be a murder, a killing of the self. The likelihood of us being asked to go on television and talk to complete strangers about the events unfolding inside our house that would lead to a suicide and a shattered family was something we did not even contemplate. The people we watched on television did not seem to belong to the same world as we did. We would never join them. We watched television, we did not think of appearing on it. We hid our feelings.

"A universe is set up by the producers according to their taste and needs. The universe is half fiction, half real, an unreal universe populated by real people. They give it rules, make a setting, cast it according to very specific guidelines as to who they think will supply the entertainment. The reality of Reality TV is that people are living in a surreal environment. Over time they become used to it and they integrate it into their lives. Then the producers make the setting meaner, more competitive, more humiliating, creating a version of reality that eventually influences our perception of what reality actually is. The cycle then continues."

Thirty two years later I appear now and then on television, possibly because I am now the grown-up version of a Stockport teenager who was a bit strange and lonely around the edges and who listened to Kevin Coyne, Faust and Peter Hammill. My father never lived to see the day when I appeared on television, although just before he died he did hear me on the radio. I talked about the local music scene in Manchester. He seemed happy to hear me but unsure of what I was actually talking about. Months later he was dead. I have never talked about his suicide on television, but then I haven't been asked, not even when I appear on daytime television.

"I just wanted to get on television. I have had a desire to be famous all my life."

We would have watched 'The Family' when it was screened in 1974, because it was on. I remember being intrigued by the fact that the streets of Reading and the clothes the family wore were not unlike the streets and clothes of Stockport. The family in 'The Family' were not like our family, apart from the fact they seemed as scruffy, and as angry, and as keen to get on with things because there was no other choice. They seemed to talk to each other and rub their lives against each other and feel some kind of love and hate. Perhaps they were behaving like this because they were on television. Perhaps it was because they were like that anyway that they were on television. They had gone through an audition period, and had been chosen to be The Family by producer Paul Watson not just because they were unorthodox and had problems, but because they were, intentionally or not, very entertaining.

The mother in the house, Margaret Wilkins, could easily have been a pal of Elsie Tanner, and the daughter, Heather, the stroppy teenager, seemed like the kind of girl that might have married a member of Slade. The Dad drove a bus around Reading with drained dignity. As they struggled through their lives, now made more complicated and yet more acceptable by the presence of cameras, they made their problems seem entertaining, or someone on their behalf did.

If the impossible had happened and a television crew took the time to film our little family over a few months, we might have ended up as loud and talkative; as explicit and entertaining. Would there have been sympathy around the country for my father, who was clearly troubled by the air that he breathed and the fact he had no money? Would they have wondered why he couldn't keep a job? Would the nation have wondered why I didn't have a girlfriend and seemed to spend all my time listening to peculiar music? Would they have noticed that I seemed to exist without socks and underwear, as my mother, presuming I was now old enough to fend for myself, had stopped buying me such things? Would my sister Jayne have been some kind of inspiration to other teenage girls for the number of boyfriends she attracted, unlike her creepy older brother, who kept himself to himself with suspicious consistency? Would my Dad have allowed the arguments he had with his wife, that sometimes lunged to the edge of violence, to be filmed? Would he have agreed to it all for money – finally finding a way to make money just being himself in the privacy of his own home, even if it did mean sacrificing that privacy?

Sometimes the family in 'The Family' seemed so real it was unreal. They were so like us, in that they looked tired, trapped and fed up, and so unlike us, in that they were on the television, approximating a position of apparent glamour, other worldly in their framed, episodic of-this-worldness. I wonder what difference it makes to your life to have such intimate film of yourself when you were just making your life up as you went along and you hadn't much of a clue about who you were and what you were like.

"Do reality TV contestants, or victims, or subjects, behave in a similar way to how people act in the real world? As with the people operating in the world of reality television, we too in most of our day-to-day behaviour are concerned with making impressions."

In the 'Radio Times', Margaret Wilkins used a diagram to show us the living arrangements in her house, which were a little unorthodox, a little less than nuclear. This was to help us understand what was going on in the Wilkins house. Headlines about the series blankly exclaimed that a new BBC series would star real people. 'The Sun' ran pieces about how Mrs Wilkins was coping with all the attention. Local MPs had things to say. The Wedding Episode caused a bit of a fuss, but it didn't seem anything to be too concerned about. There were people who appeared on TV and made their living that way, and people who appeared on TV – like the contestants in 'The Generation Game' – who didn't. There was no sign at the time that the two sides would ever really get mixed up. How could that possibly happen?

It would take another quarter of a century before observational television in the socio-political tradition was fully mutated by the commercial pressure to entertain. It took a long time after the isolated incident of 'The Family' before the seriousness of the documentary was irreversibly combined with the frivolity of the soap, unified by the need to package particular aspects of daily life as entertainment.By the end of the 20th century, the broadcasting imperative was to attract peak-time audiences for factual series at a minimal cost, to deliver ratings on a low budget, which essentially meant following ordinary people in their ordinary lives – learning to drive, working at a vets or singing on a cruise ship – and making documentaries in the style of a soap. No actors or stars were needed, and no scriptwriters, which kept down costs. Within a few years of these types of shows being broadcast, the headlines were exclaiming: 'Who Needs Talent?', 'It's All Down Hill From Here' and 'How Low Will Reality TV Go?'

"How real can someone's actions actually be when they know they are being filmed? Really real, or not really real at all, or sort of both?"

Was 'The Family' the very start of what is now known as Reality Television? It was certainly one of the starts, a key point on the way to all British television being essentially a kind of variation on reality TV, as if that is what it has been all along.

To find the source of reality television you can look to the American show 'Candid Camera' in the 1950s, which famously and rather sweetly 'caught people in the act of being themselves'. Reality television began in America, in the optimistic, protected 1950s, just like rock'n'roll. It was a time when people were just getting used to television, and so programming was pleasant, uncomplicated and not at all controversial. Television became more explicit and extreme during the Sixties, a time when assassinations and wars happened live on television. Entertainment became more swinging, challenging and twisted to keep up with the reality it was editing to shape. Openness replaced modesty as a virtue; independence was more important than privacy.

In the early Seventies, 'An American Family' revealed how there were people quite happy to expose themselves on television, as if this was the only way for them to feel complete, as if they were more comfortable talking about themselves on TV than to their family, or their neighbours, or their priest. Bill and Pat Loud's marriage was breaking up. Their son Lance announced he was gay. The Louds allowed all this to be filmed, and edited into weekly entertainment.

The young television producer Paul Watson, a conscientious controversialist, took this idea, and created 'The Family', anticipating well ahead of his time that the British could be as available, as self-flagellating, as garrulous and needy, as weirdly honest, as the Americans. He considered himself a documentary maker. For him 'The Family' was about giving a voice to people usually overlooked, even if this voice was ultimately in his hands, and to some extent put through his mouth.'Documentary film must question the status quo,' he said. 'You can only do that if you speak to ordinary people, not politicians. People need to understand one another better.'

He didn't consider that there was a danger that he would patronise the Wilkins, negatively influence their lives, leave them in ruins while he went on to his next project. He had the best of intentions. 'There is no point simply going out to take the piss out of society.' He was just a little step short of discovering the magical equation – where ordinary people and everyday lives are combined with the discipline and demands of televised show business, reality itself is changed, and TV has unimagined new power to probe and control this new reality. His main concern, perhaps, was to show people as they really were, even as he acknowledged that it was impossible to do such a thing, because as soon as people are filmed, and watched, and photographed, they cease to be who they really are, and become something else. He wanted to film a document of family life in the early Seventies, to help write history. The history he ended up writing was more to do with the history of television than the history of the family.

After 'The Family', ordinary people, the non-famous, direct from their everyday homes, appeared on television more and more, but usually their role was still limited to one-off appearances on quiz shows, and these appearances didn't lead to the cover of 'TV Times' or Page 3 in 'The Sun'. 'It's A Knockout' was an early, silly sign of reality television as a combination of competition and humiliation. Contestants on Cilla Black's 'Blind Date' had a little run at experiencing a dose of fame, at flexing their amateur talent to amuse, but very much trapped inside the show's quaint rules. Celebrities weren't in any way yet required to imitate the desperate behaviour of non-celebrities in order to keep hold of viewers' attention.

It was MTV's 'Real World' that pioneered the idea of arranging the lives of ordinary people for the sake of entertainment, without falling back on an increasingly old-fashioned defence that they were doing so for some vaguely beneficial sociological reasons. This was playing with people's hopes and dreams for pure fun. They put strangers in the same environment for a certain length of time, set up psychological clashes, created stress and pressure, and watched what happened. They treated the ensuing drama as you would fiction, supplying an emotion-enhancing soundtrack, shaping each episode into an easily understandable narrative with the help of confessions and complaints from the volunteers/victims. Scriptwriters, and presenters, had been replaced, and whatever script there was emerged in an improvised state.

Having invented most of the rules of what would become reality television, America exported the idea, and saw it eventually sent back in a new improved form – a kind of TV equivalent of the British pop invasion in the 1960s. 'Changing Rooms' gently introduced the idea of the self-improvement and the makeover, and a programme conceived in Britain that debuted in Sweden as 'Expedition Robinson', eventually to be known around the world as 'Survivor', developed the idea of the competition, and the weekly elimination of contestants until a winner remained. By the end of the 20th century, reality television was either in the docu-soap form, where there was a hint of some kind of acknowledgement of the serious, life-enhancing roots of documentary making, or the game show form, which was a carefully engineered competition that spliced together manufactured factual elements with psychological and physical tests, talk show elements lifted from the world of Donahue and Springer, and a basic commitment to entertainment values.

And then, just in time for the 21st century, to confirm that this was no trend but a serious new genre, out of Holland, and then out of Channel 4, part serious experiment, part slapstick entertainment, part hip, part trash, came the perfectly named 'Big Brother'.

"I don't know what the appeal of 'Big Brother' is. In my day there were proper programmes with real plots and characters. I watched this 'Big Brother' and it was like when I was home with my family. Except that we only lived in a two-bedroom terraced house and there were nine of us."

I have no idea why my father killed himself – perhaps I should discuss it with Trisha in front of a live studio audience – but he certainly removed himself at about the time that television really started to become a member of the family, and, more than that, started to be the leader of the family: a source of religious, commercial, sexual and psychological power; a combination of church, theatre, health centre, advice bureau, school, sports stadium, hotel, art gallery, strip club, casino, estate agent, bank, decorator and, to some extent, parent.

He died in the 1970s, when really the telly was just the telly, where people did telly things, in a telly way, and the telly was set to the side of real life, not embedded right inside it, part of its very tissue and muscle. Factual television was intended to be informative, and enquiring, and to some extent educational, but it wasn't really a place where you could learn, directly and indirectly, to be a chef, pop star, ballroom dancer, ice skater, model, fashion designer, millionaire, soldier, stylist, TV presenter, acrobat, gambler, interior designer, teacher, boxer, hairdresser… and ultimately, celebrity, and beyond that, has-been. More and more routes to appearing on television have opened up, and more and more people are quite prepared to take those routes even if some of them lead to profound embarrassment or even some form of torture. For more and more people, appearing on television helps them make sense of their lives, as if this is where they find out who they are, as if you're no one until you're on TV.

Appearing on television hasn't as yet helped me make sense of my life, although it has helped me make sense of television, and some of its power. I suppose I was keen to start appearing on television because I was curious to find out if it would make a difference to my life, to see if it would make me feel special, or more noticed.

The American novelist John Updike once said that when you appear on television you are yourself, but more so, and this is true. You can become addicted to this feeling, and you also notice a difference in the way that other people treat you. It is as if appearing on television helps other people make sense of who you are. They can place you. You are to an extent a familiar part of their immediate surroundings, a kind of comfort. In a way you become a part of their family, and they feel that they know you. This can considerably boost your self-esteem. There are those prepared to go to some length in order to appear on television and experience this enhancement of self-confidence, to become a part of this exclusive virtual family. Those eager to appear on television who are not generally the type of professionals who would be on television because of some skill or experience feel that appearing on television means that they can prove to the rest of the world that they have arrived, that they are someone, that they are good at something. Only by appearing on television can you explain to the rest of the world that you are who you are.

"It's a psychological experiment being shared live with the whole of the country, or mindless TV for sad people who have no life of their own."

Gene Simmons, the Cheeky Girls and Maggot sing happy birthday to Jeff Brazier. Kerry Katona collapses in a sponsored heap. Someone from 'Wife Swap' swaps numbers with Jade Goody's mum. Trisha Goddard explains with terrific certainty that what she is interested in is conflict and resolution. Maureen from 'Driving School' arm-wrestles with Twiggy. George Michael falls asleep. Jane McDonald spanks a naked Ralf Little. Ruby Wax smiles as if this will solve all of the world's problems. The son of George Best is kissing a girl who a moment ago was screaming out that 'some things are private'. Nick Bateman, now known as Nasty Nick for sensationally breaking the rules on 'Big Brother' season 1, is telling Norman Mailer that 'I was just an ordinary guy who took part in an unusual experiment amidst considerable scrutiny.' Mailer confides that 'I'm not opposed to reality programming ipso facto. Out of the crucible of improvisation great things can emerge. It just depends who is in charge.' I swear I hear a woman who became a television personality through her expertise as a cleaner tell Little Jimmy Osmond 'If you are on television enough in a novel set of circumstances you can become a kind of celebrity and your reality can change.' Chantelle reads out pages from her autobiography. Heather is interviewed by Trisha as an ordinary grown-up woman who never got the chance to write a best-seller about the few months she was framed on television and how the rest of her life was changed because of it. A young girl watches the television as if she's learning something about life, about who she is, as if she is part of a mysterious, insidious experiment she'll spend her life trying to understand, as if reality begins and ends on the screen.

"Characters are created that have nothing to do with actual personality through editing techniques that transform hours of boring footage into conflict or tragedy. Such manipulation of mundane moments and the creation of narrative using what is almost found material can provide suspense that conventional narrative has difficulty in matching."

I looked around the room filled with people I had watched on television exposing themselves, who had spent considerable television hours inventing, rescuing or destroying their careers. All these people had various claims to fame, from masturbating pigs on Channel 5 to failing to impress the entrepreneur Sir Alan Sugar enough to win a job in his company. Some of them only seemed to exist as characters that appeared on television shows that were created in order to humiliate and embarrass celebrities who weren't in fact famous for anything other than appearing on shows where they displayed their lack of fame as if this was a sign of fame. They were somehow famous for not being famous, which then gets translated as being famous for being famous. One or two in the room could claim to have slept with Princess

Diana. One or two of them once worked for Princess Diana. Was Diana's appearance on 'Panorama' where she opened her heart with ruthless precision another influence on the eventual shape and texture of reality television?

A few of them in the room had once been famous for having done something, in sport or pop or comedy, but now they were forced to spend their time in rooms like this finding whatever ways they could to remind whoever was interested that they were once really famous for doing something that involved some kind of skill, or talent, or vision. A small magician and his even smaller wife who seemed to share their hair sat next to an alcoholic ex footballer and a model who once had an affair with a television presenter who got sacked because of his addiction to cocaine. Someone who once knew Benny from 'Crossroads' chatted amiably with someone who had launched their career on the back of once selling a disgraced politician a condom.

All of us were in the room waiting to go onto a television show to speak our mind for seconds at a time, for which we were being paid a nominal sum. It was possible that we were all really there in order to publicise ourselves. Our job was to publicise our ability to publicise ourselves in a world trained to believe that the only way to get on was to be noticed by enough people to make it seem as if your life had real purpose. Together we represented, as well as we could, for better or worse, a world as shaped by television that was infatuated with surgical enhancement, diet, hair extensions, self-publicity, gadgets, gossip and the general appearance of celebrities.

"We were aware of the cameras at first but after a while they became part of the family."

As I sat squeezed behind the running mouths and sore opinionated might of Vanessa Feltz and John McCririck as part of what could be described as a celebrity audience waiting to greet the participants at the climax of the 2006 celebrity edition of 'Big Brother', I couldn't help but wonder how on earth:

(a) I had got there.

(b) Any of us in the studio had got there: a fee, a scandal, an ego, a travesty, an insincerity, a desperation, an ache, a need, a weakness, a red carpet, a facelift, a shame of extremely minor celebrities crammed into a room ready to be roundly ribbed and roasted by the host, modern Byronic buffoon Russell Brand. Randy Brand, the saucy stand-up De Sade, the missing link between Lenny Bruce and Jerry Springer, addicted to his own way with words, to the ghostly surprise of his own torn thoughts, to his own way of bending his wired, hairy body around space and time like he was trying to swap one for the other, would prod us with a long silver microphone, needling us to say something damned near coherent inside ten burning seconds while we were being watched by those who didn't care less what we had to say.

(c) Television itself had got there, into this position where the winner of the 2006 'Big Brother' celebrity edition was in fact not as such a celebrity, or at least had not been one when she went into the house. Chantelle, the winner of 'Celebrity Big Brother' 2006, had entered the house more or less as an ordinary person, someone who didn't appear on television, or on the cover of magazines, or as someone who doesn't sell the photographs of their wedding to a gossip magazine for hundreds of thousands of pounds. She came out of the house after a few weeks of manipulated pretence, intrigue, romance and chaos as the celebrity winner, as a celebrity who would spend the following months being treated by the media and the nation's television audience as if she really was a star, someone of note, someone with literal charisma. Inside the house she had fallen, or was pushed, or just answered the question correctly, into a relationship with the character that had been put inside as the edgy, subversive pop star, Samuel Preston, whose stage name is Preston in the way that Steven Morrissey's stage name is Morrissey. Pleasant and vaguely enigmatic, he had entered the house apparently engaged to another woman, but destiny, as decided by materialistically mystical televisual powers, meant that he was doomed to be lured into the Chantelle fairy story, and be steered, as if no one or no one thing was doing the steering, into a passive role as Prince Charming. (They were to be married – and this would make Chantelle's new name Chantelle Preston. Presumably Preston would be Preston Chantelle. Fans christened them Prestelle.)

The brave, handsome Preston and the gay, delightful Chantelle fell in love live on television; dated, danced and dreamed for the grubby, manipulative small screen. Their calculated game show love match, this mutant romance made in HD heaven, was surrounded by a sweat, a death, a vanity, a shallow pool of celebrities looking on in televised helplessness knowing that however famous they had been or could be again, however brittle their emotions, however catastrophic their confessions, however exuberant their behaviour, they could not beat this young fresh girl with her blinding smile representing clean, spiritual novelty.

She had been nothing, no one, not on television, not in the gossip news, not needed by the paparazzi, not special in any way, and now, while they watched, she was becoming fame. She was changing from dead common and entirely ordinary into a smiling, endlessly charming creature designed by greed, fate, agents and the lust of a nation set up to be transfixed. Her smile, the distance between her hands and her legs, the connection between her soul and her need to shop for shoes, it had all been measured and found to be perfect. She was made out to be famous live on television so that within weeks the real celebrities she shared the house with, the girl herself, and everyone who was watching and voting, believed that she was famous. We were all involved in the process of turning an unknown into a known someone as if it had been a kind of modern miracle we were all responsible for. We had, so it seemed, power, to make and break and design the world.

(d) Television had reached the state of Chantelle, the newly crowned queen of reality TV, reality defined as that which mocks, buys, sells, parodies, savages, reduces, cleans, rewrites, fixes and manipulates the idea of reality as the one thing that holds us all together, TV defined as that thing which runs our lives even if we've got better things to do than watch it, make it or appear on it.

"We have seen a steady increase in the appetite for programmes that approximate real human responses because advances in technology ultimately create more and more isolation between people."

As a member of this pit, this pathétique, this champagne, this studio, this despair, this small talk, this limousine of monstrously minor celebrities, I was going to be one of the first outsiders allowed to greet Chantelle on her return to the real world. She was coming back to life with a new life, as if her story had been written by a combination of Boyd Hilton, Angela Carter and Walt Disney. The show started, live on E4, later to be shown on Channel 4. The warp, the damage, the strain of celebrities invited to welcome the prize-winning Chantelle and her new partner in fantasy Preston waited for the moment Russell would thrust his slender silver microphone towards them and ask for their views.

Chantelle sat on her own chair in the middle of the studio, a golden throne explicitly positioned under a grabbing spotlight. Her fellow contestants, including a Welsh comedy rapper, a 'Baywatch' actress and the disgraced light entertainer Michael Barrymore, sat in a row in front of the audience, the has-been, the vacuum, the party, of invited celebrities. I was sat behind Barrymore, who, not alone amongst the inmates who had just emerged from the 'Big Brother' house just a few yards away from where we were sat, clearly did not know:

(a) Where he was.

(b) What day it was.

(c) Why he had lost to someone he had never heard of when his fame had once been enough to make him as famous as anyone in the land.

(d) What was happening.

(e) Who I was and what reality show I might have appeared on that would make me qualified enough to greet them as they emerged from one planet and dropped abruptly onto another; but perhaps I was there as some kind of expert in suicide.

(f) Whether there had been any point in suffering these few weeks inside the 'Big Brother' house in order to try and repair a career that was essentially beyond repair.

(g) That I had intended on this special occasion, as soon as Russell planted his vulgar sliver of metal into my face on live TV, that my words would be a quote from Aldous Huxley. As Chantelle sat melting from nameless no-one into one-name someone just a few feet ahead of me, as her brand-new boyfriend mustered up frayed neo-indie cool amidst this near hysterical circus, as the plug of celebrities hustled and shifted all around me, as Russell sat in my lap and demanded on live television some sort of instant response to the Cinderella victory of the lovely Chantelle and/or the grim loss of Barrymore, as Gillian Wearing watched from a safe distance and calculated just how far television and identity had come since 1974, I was going to say:

'I think that the truth, and by that I mean The Truth, has been drowned in a sea of irrelevance. As Huxley taught us, in the age of advanced technology, spiritual devastation is more likely to come from an enemy with a smiling face rather than one whose countenance evokes suspicion and hate. In the Huxley prophecy, Big Brother does not watch us, by his choice. We watch him, by our choice.' It would not be clear if I was accusing the fresh-smelling, ecstatically smiling Chantelle herself of being some sinister front, a false God, invented in front of our eyes, as if there was no foul play, to convince a spellbound nation all was well in the face of rot and ruin. It might, though, cause the sub-celebrities around me to riot. They had been gathered to baptise the new born Chantelle into their ranks, brought to Brand's Church of Freaks to snip the umbilical cord that connected this glowing bouncing example of baby fame to the pre-celebrity womb, to the floating void that there is before you are famous. They would have reacted badly if I'd suggested that Chantelle was some sort of anti-Christ — not the incandescent innocent princess but the sly wicked witch. I was prepared to speak my mind, which wasn't quite convinced that 'Heat' magazine ruled the world, that reality TV was merely harmless knockabout escapist fun. Perhaps it was this tendency that had made me enough of a TV freak to be invited to sit amongst this eccentricity of celebrities.

The bright, brutal Russell, though, was only expecting a few words from me. To say anything negative or doubtful would under the circumstances have seemed churlish. To say anything that took longer than a couple of short breaths would have been pornographically impertinent. The point at this ceremony was to offer a gift, and swiftly say something admiring. There would be no time for me to speak for more than ten seconds, no opportunity for me to wonder aloud just how it came to be that Chantelle, representing reality TV, was exactly what television was invented for. She fits perfectly the artistic capabilities of the medium, I would say, to a snort from McCririck, and an iffy expletive from someone who made their fame courting the step-daughter of Paul Gascoigne on what has become known as the love island.

No time for me to begin to explore where this story had all begun. Just what was the once upon a time that had led to Chantelle? How had we got from Heather Wilkins to Chantelle? From worthy social experiment to materialistic entertainment experiment? Would young girls find Chantelle as inspiring, as intriguing, as some young girls had found the feisty, opinionated Heather? Did it say a lot about the difference between 1974 and 2006 that Heather spoke her mind, was fighting for her rights, and Chantelle didn't really have much on her mind, other than fame, and romance, and clothes, and make-up.

I said something quick and inoffensive before Russell snatched away his glistening elongated pole and offered it to Edwina Currie and Abi Titmuss. Chantelle momentarily directed the candy-coloured smile of the ultimate reality winner right at me. I was for a spiralling split-second completely dazzled by the psychedelic power of reality television to make over people and change their lives. She was reality itself, alive with the moment, living a life on live television, defined by the screen, and the story she had been given to act out by shadowy powers that be... And just as I was about to make this claim on live television, as if I too could experience this transcendent reality only achieved when your life coincides with live television, Russell sprang into the orbit of some other expert in the audience. I would have to wait until I could catch his raving roving eye again, and this time I was determined to use the occasion to map out how television had gone from, say, 'Candid Camera' to Chantelle, from 'Blind Date' to Chantelle and Preston, from Heather Wilkins, 'The Family's outspoken teenager who got to live a life on TV when there was no reality TV, just observational documentary, to Chantelle, 'Big Brother's non-celebrity celebrity who was invented on television which was invented for just such invention.

"We should understand the reality TV phenomenon in terms of a repression of moral questions which day-to-day life poses, but which are denied answers."

Russell never gave me a chance to say anything else to the precious Chantelle, possibly because he could sense I was about to launch into a rant of freakish length that was filled with the poison of speculation and meaning. Six months later, as the story of Chantelle and Preston continued in an outside world increasingly dominated by the faces and actions of crude cut-out celebrities, as the Primark Monroe professionally went through the motions of living happily ever after with her Cecil Gee Brando, I found myself sat in the same Brand-dominated studio. I was surrounded by some of the same celebrities. This time we were gathered to welcome the winner, runners-up and losers of 'Big Brother' series 7. Series 7 had also managed to produce a romance, between two people, Pete and Nikki, so differently damaged that there was no way that they belonged together. This was either very funny, or very sad. Their romance was not destined to end with a strategically timed wedding that ended up on the cover of 'OK', but with Nikki losing the will to live, or at least eat.

As usual, the 'Big Brother' series had produced a collection of stories that, once you were hooked, were impossible to ignore. You had to find out how they ended, however appalling the characters involved, however trivial the story, just in case how things resolved offered some clue to the nature of your own life, how you might deal with your own problems. In front of me sat Pete – the winner, twitching, cursing and blanking out on Chantelle's throne – Richard, Grace, Nikki, Aisleyne, Glyn, Imogen, Lea and Mikey. They still seemed like the semi-fictional characters they'd been inside the house, not quite real, people you could insult and patronise because being inside the television they didn't seem to have feelings, even as all they did was expose their feelings. I'd hated some of these people when they were in the house, on the television for hours at a time doing nothing much but eat, breathe and bitch. In front of me, intoxicated by the speed of which things were happening to them, they seemed suddenly almost human, trapped on their lonely journey to various kinds of pointless provisional fame.

Russell stamped through all this human wreckage with a bitter glee bordering on show business violence. He was hunting sensation and chaos, with the keen eye of someone who himself was hunted, for exploitable signs of breakdown, of unusual vulnerability. He was now by far the most famous person in the room, peering down on the feeble of minor celebrities that snapped at his rock and roll ankles for some attention, amused by the 'Big Brother' contestants who had a look in their eye that suggested they complacently thought their dream of fame was already satisfied. Through his degraded will alone this live show filled with the messy energy of faded celebrities, hardy celebrities and brand-new celebrities stopped just short of descending into a mess of narcissism and bickering.

He noticed me trying to draw him towards me away from his position in between Jade Goody and Jodie Marsh, where he was happy to make a sordid nuisance of himself. He gave me a look that warned me away from trying any funny business that involved reasonable behaviour and considered thought, and swooped right into the heart of my space. The point was to simply honour Pete as the winner, and sprinkle some cheerful words of appreciation over his frantic brow. He had been voted the winner by the people, and to question this result would under the circumstances seem sinister, and possibly in some form quite fundamentalist.

Russell squeezed between me and the man who had cheated on 'Who Wants To Be A Millionaire'. His skinny magic wand hovered near my mouth. This meant I was on live television surrounded by freshly minted 'Big Brother' celebrities destined to have their lives fondled over by a public trained to demand instant gratification. Richard, the only gay who lasted in the house, and Nikki, the tantrum tyrant, turned round to see if they recognised me, and looked disappointed that I wasn't Philip Schofield or Wayne Sleep.

I wanted to make some sort of serious point, possibly about the connection between private and public spheres of existence, possibly about the connection between Pete's time on television and the time Heather Wilkins spent over thirty years ago when an appearance on television by an ordinary person didn't automatically lead to a life in show business, even if the ordinary person was controversial, loud-mouthed, worked-up and entertainingly damaged. I wanted to talk about how the chase for revelation had taken us from 'The Family' to 'Big Brother', how we were all implicated in the way this need to know who we were and what was to come of us had led to such cruel, irresistible entertainment. Russell was quickly alert to how my body position indicated I was about to be potentially serious. He made some remark about my testicles, which lacked something essential in his opinion, and snatched his slender stick away from my mouth just before I got a chance to say to Pete the winner: 'It's not so much that everyone will be famous for fifteen minutes but that nowadays there is a new famous person produced every fifteen minutes.'

Brand leapt away from me in one fluid movement straight into the silky lap of Trisha Goddard, where he confessed his sins, explained his motives, sobbed a little and felt better for doing it all in public. 'None of this is real,' I started to shout: 'It's just television!'

But it was no good. The microphone was somewhere else. No one could hear me.

LIFE is a lot quieter now at the home of the famous Wilkins family —"The Family" of BBC TV.

As the last programme is due to appear tomorrow, they all have different feelings about the way weekly TV exposure has touched their lives in Reading, Berks.

Mother, Margaret Wilkins, says: "I'm 40 next February and life should begin then for me, shouldn't it? That's what they say." Meanwhile, she's now often alone with the dog, cat and kitten, the budgie and the goldfish.

Dad, bus-driver Terry, says "The

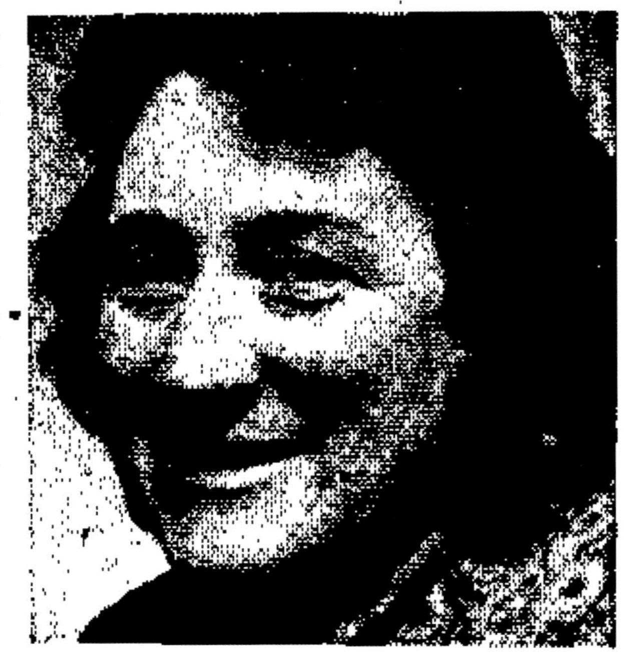

Family mum: criticised

The Family to fame

MARGARET WILKINS leans on her kitchen sink and tries hard not to light another cigarette. She's trying to break the habit, again.

"I only do interviews professionally, now," she says.

"I have a newspaper column and we have been on the radio several times. It's not that we've made a lot of money from TV.

"The wedding, the holiday in Majorca — both seen by viewers — and the second-hand car

was and that's the main thing. Anyway, he is Terry's son by adoption.

"I'm glad to say nobody has said a word about that to Christo-

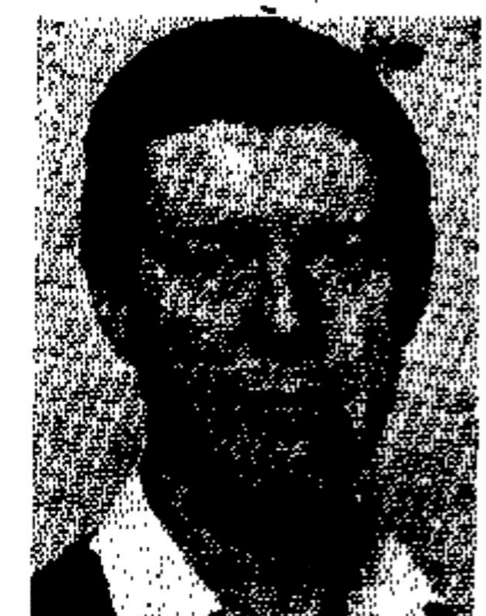

DAD: hates whispers.

passengers have a laugh and a joke about me sometimes. One man got on at Oxford and asked me, 'Who's that woman who plays your wife?'

...mily is closer than ever before."

...And that despite the fact that ...ly teenaged daughter Heather ...d younger brother Christopher ...e still living with them (apart ...om the family zoo).

...Son Gary, daughter-in-law Karen ...d their baby, Scott, have gone to ...council flat. Marian and lodger ...m Bernes no longer live upstairs. ...ey also have a flat of their own ...ce their much-publicised wedding.

...The BBC crew left them three ...eks ago. And the family miss ...em. Now that they are just ...ople again, they feel EMPTY . . .

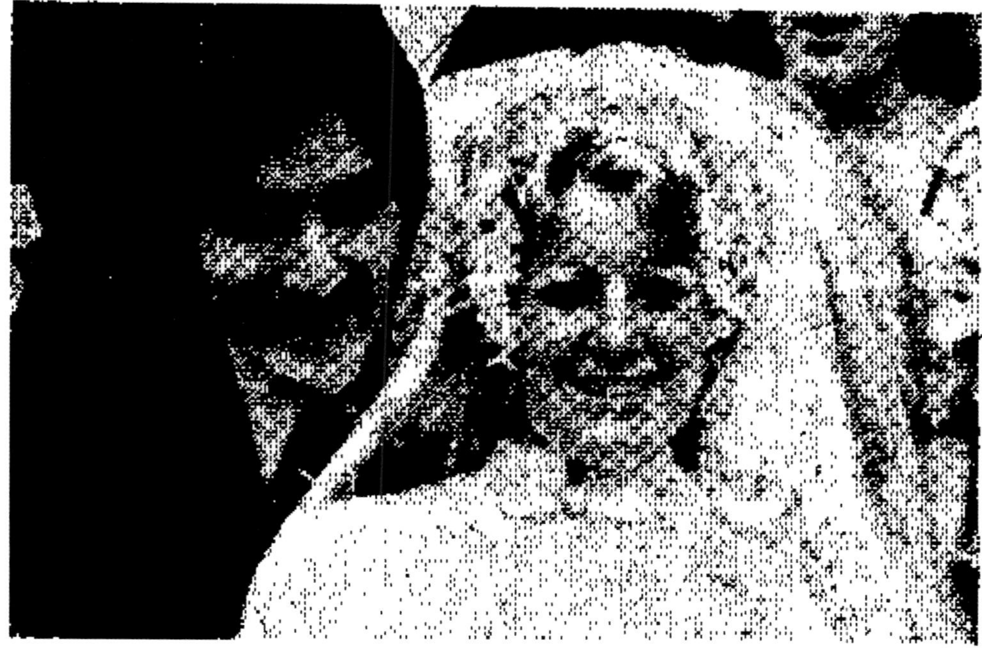
Family wedding: ordeal for Marian and Tom.

says farewell

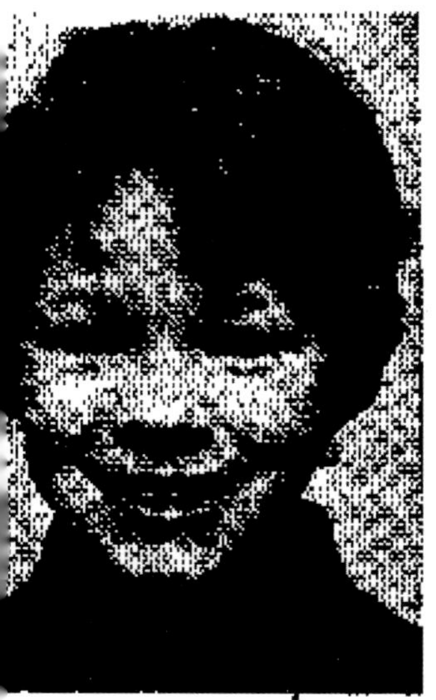
...ristopher: so funny.

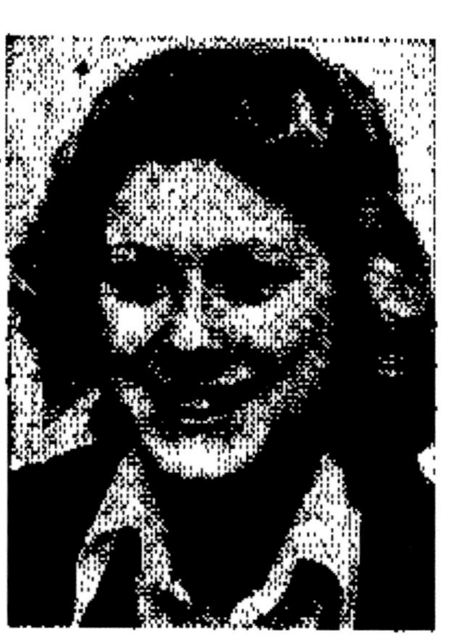
Heather: sorry it's over.

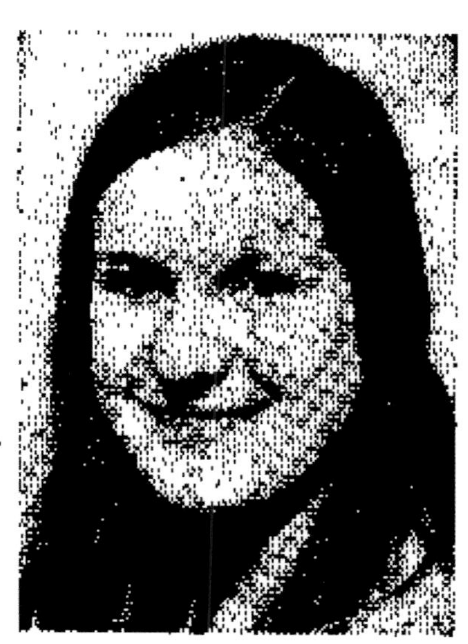
Karen: problem solved.

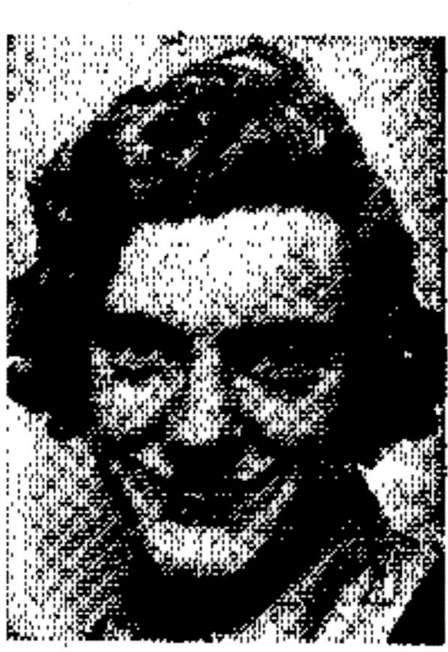
Gary: learned respect.

...'s phone-in, but we ...d for two."

...RIAN, ...he hairdresser and

us. But I haven't changed and I am not drinking gin and tonic in the saloon bar.

"I still like my brown ...d mild."

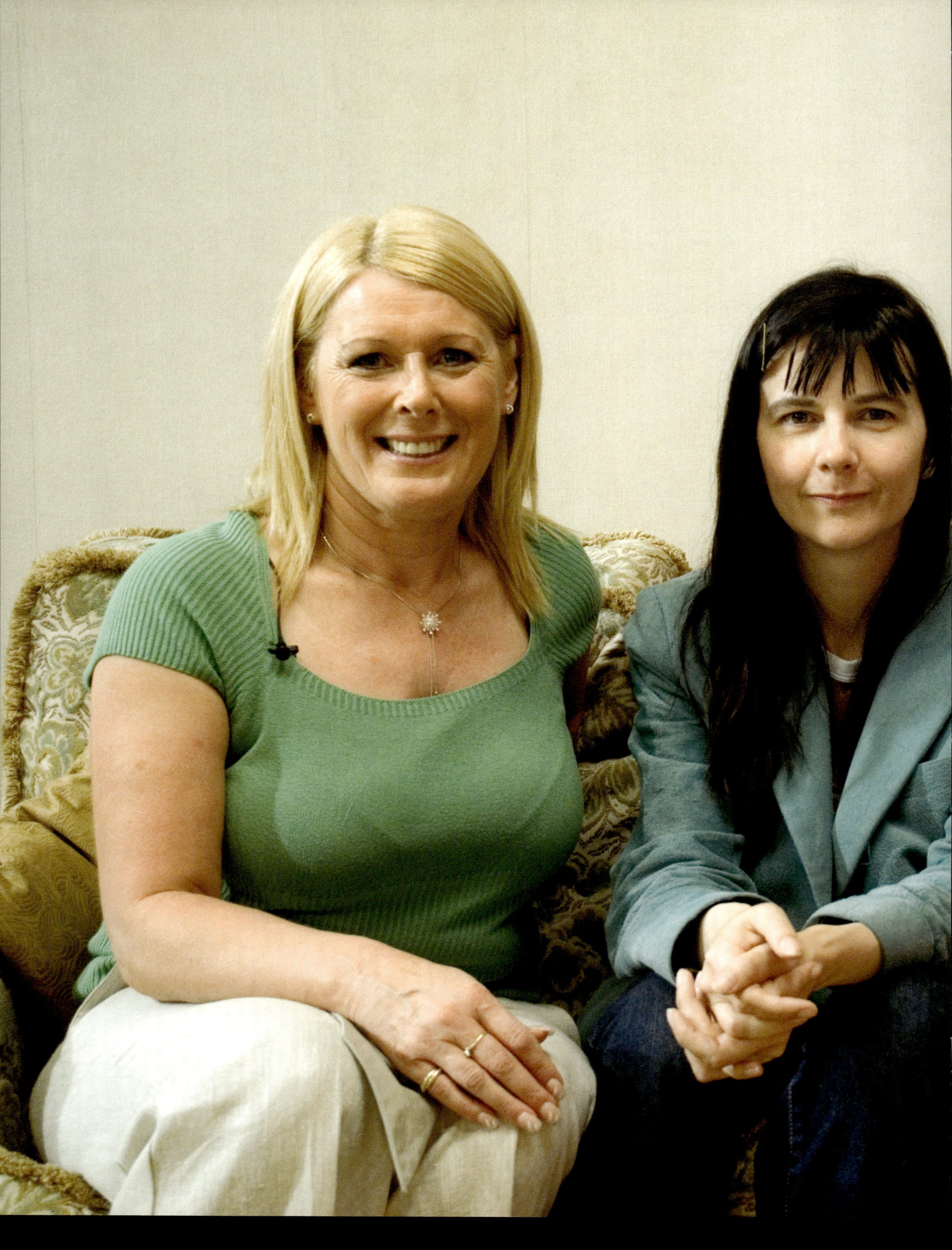

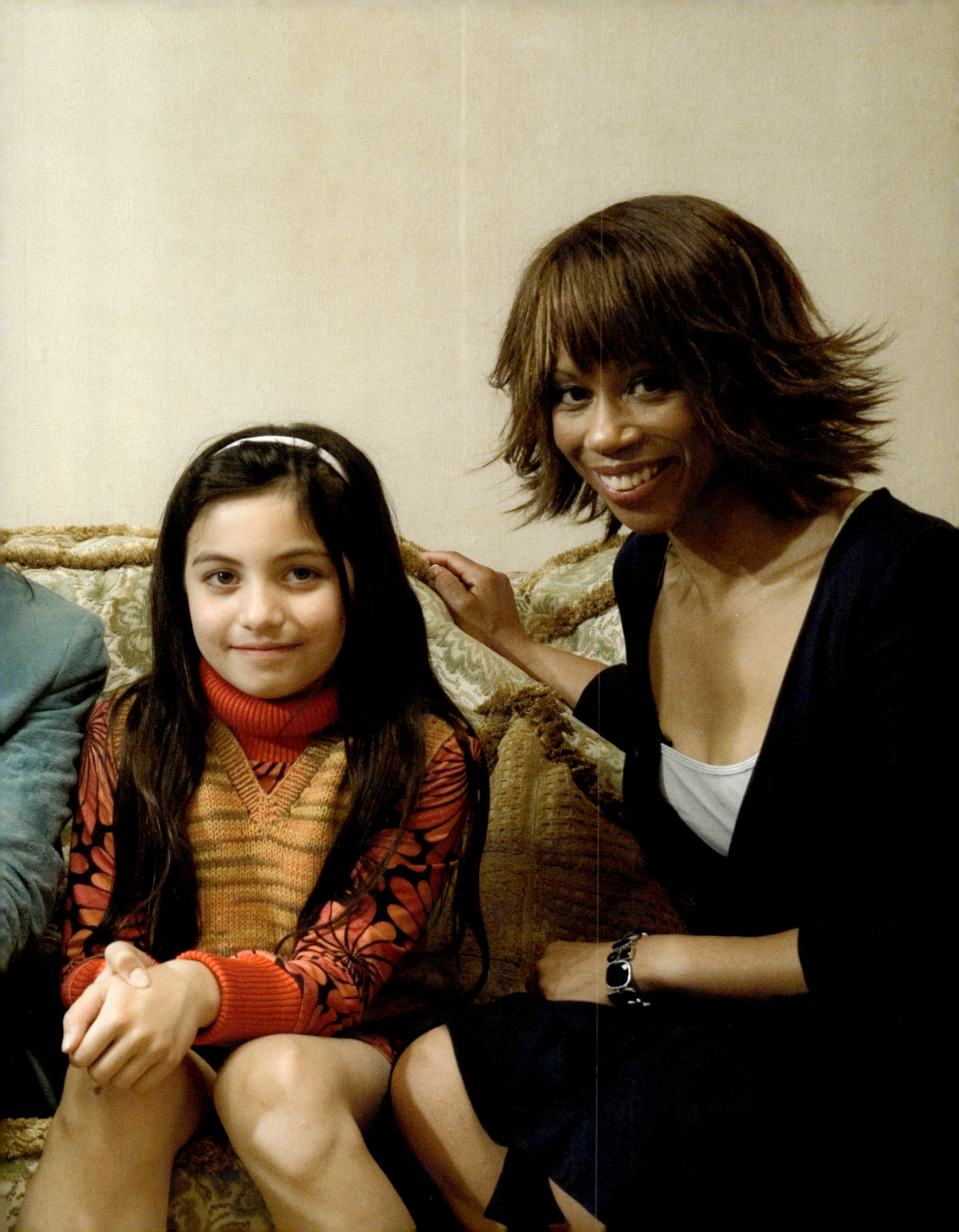

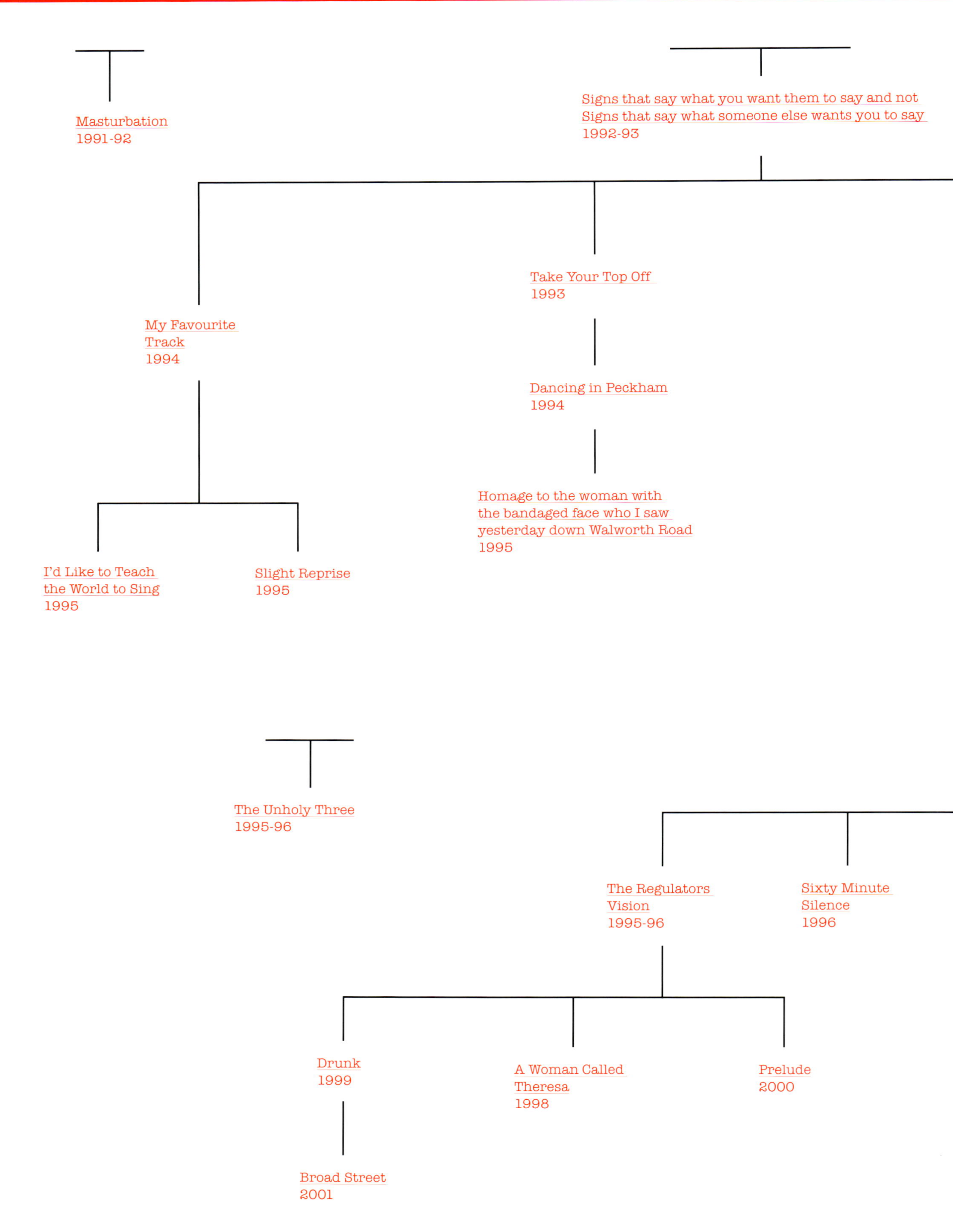

Masturbation
1991-92

Signs that say what you want them to say and not
Signs that say what someone else wants you to say
1992-93

My Favourite
Track
1994

Take Your Top Off
1993

Dancing in Peckham
1994

I'd Like to Teach
the World to Sing
1995

Slight Reprise
1995

Homage to the woman with
the bandaged face who I saw
yesterday down Walworth Road
1995

The Unholy Three
1995-96

The Regulators
Vision
1995-96

Sixty Minute
Silence
1996

Drunk
1999

A Woman Called
Theresa
1998

Prelude
2000

Broad Street
2001

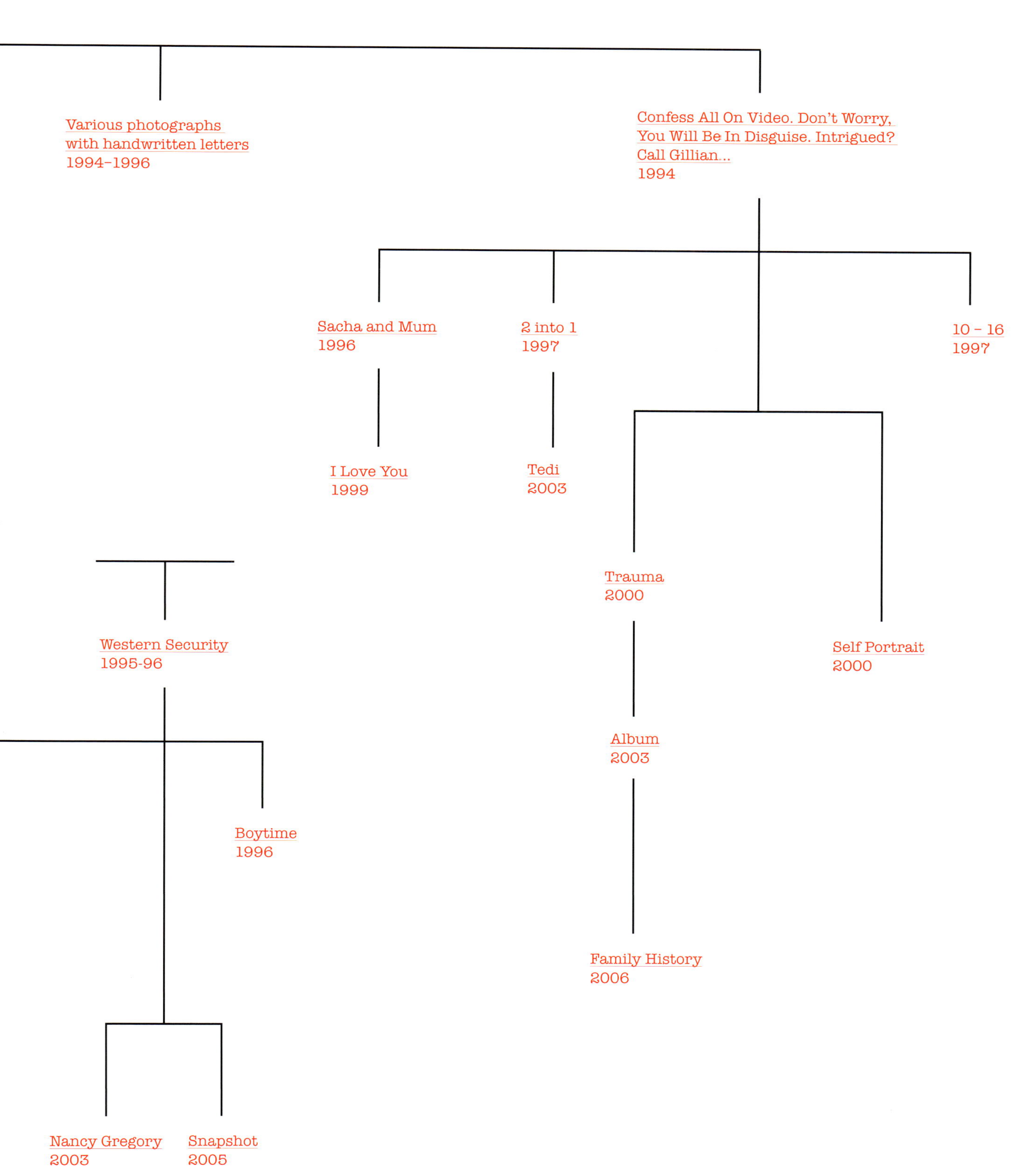
Various photographs
with handwritten letters
1994–1996

Confess All On Video. Don't Worry,
You Will Be In Disguise. Intrigued?
Call Gillian…
1994

Sacha and Mum
1996

2 into 1
1997

10 – 16
1997

I Love You
1999

Tedi
2003

Trauma
2000

Self Portrait
2000

Western Security
1995-96

Boytime
1996

Album
2003

Family History
2006

Nancy Gregory
2003

Snapshot
2005

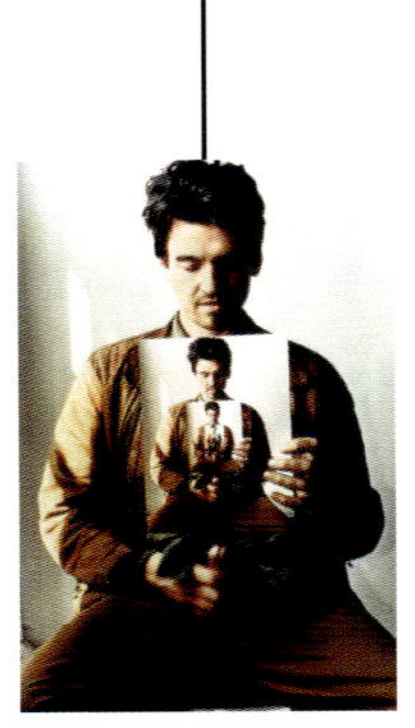

Masturbation
c-type print
1991-92

Take Your Top Off
c-type prints
1993

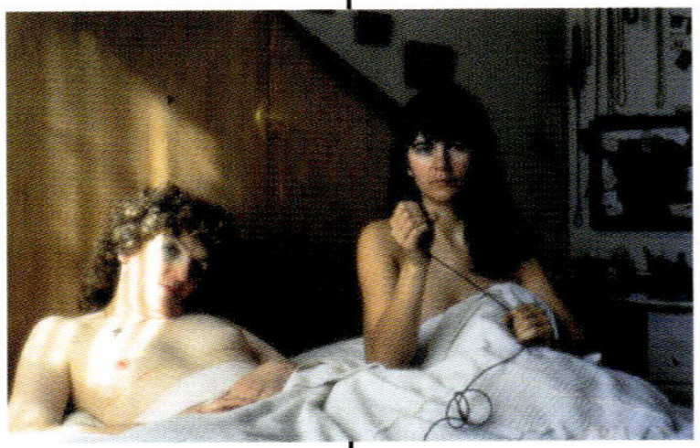

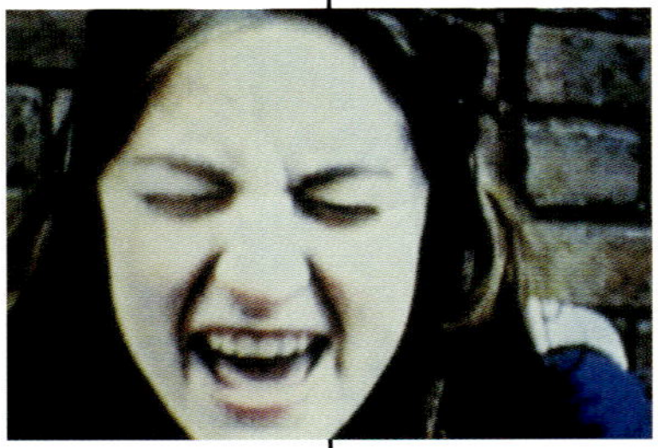

My Favourite Track
5 monitor installation
with sound
1994

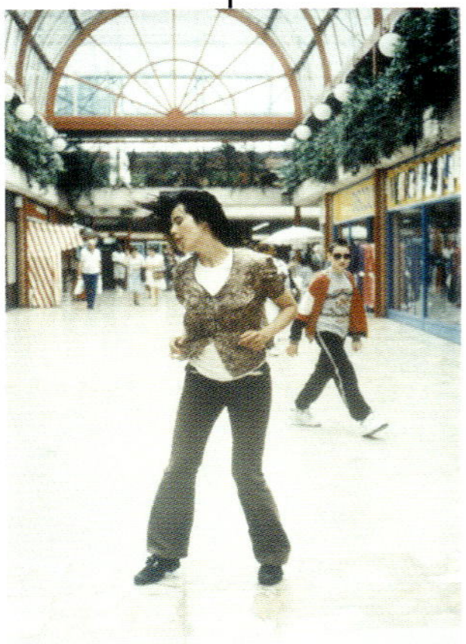

Dancing in
Peckham
video
25 minutes
1994

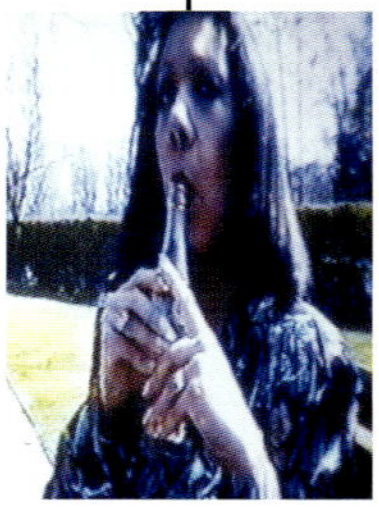

I'd Like to Teach the
World to Sing
projection with sound
1 minute 49 seconds
1995

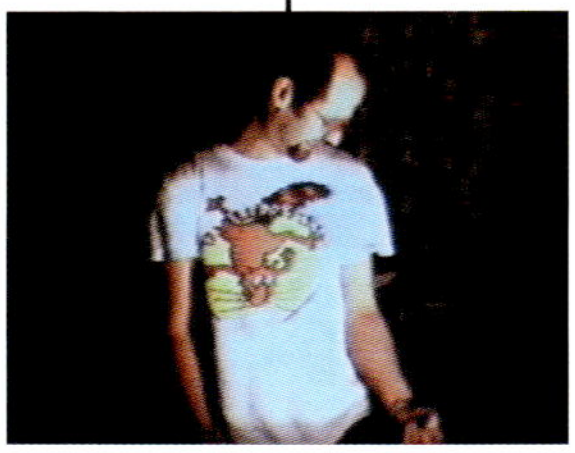

Slight Reprise
projection
17 minutes
1995

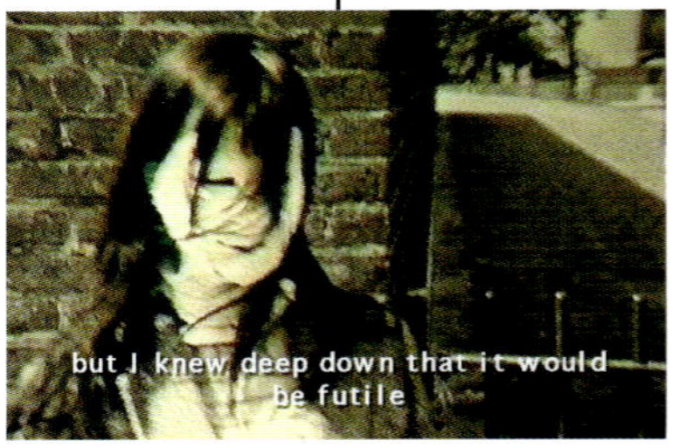

Homage to the woman with the bandaged face
who I saw yesterday down Walworth Road
black and white, and colour video projection
with subtitles
7 minutes
1995

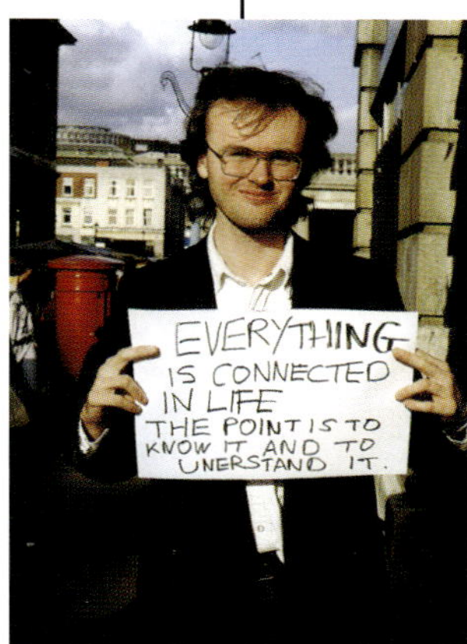

Signs that say what you want them
to say and not Signs that say what
someone else wants you to say

Including (left):
Everything is connected in life.
The point is to know it and to
understand it.
c-type print
1992-93

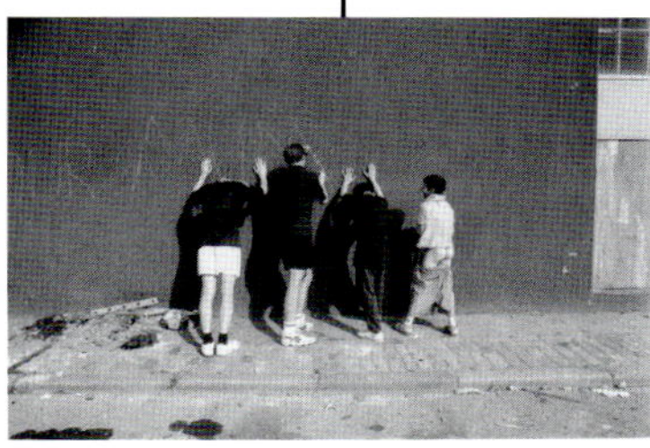
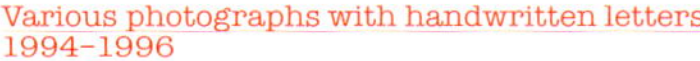
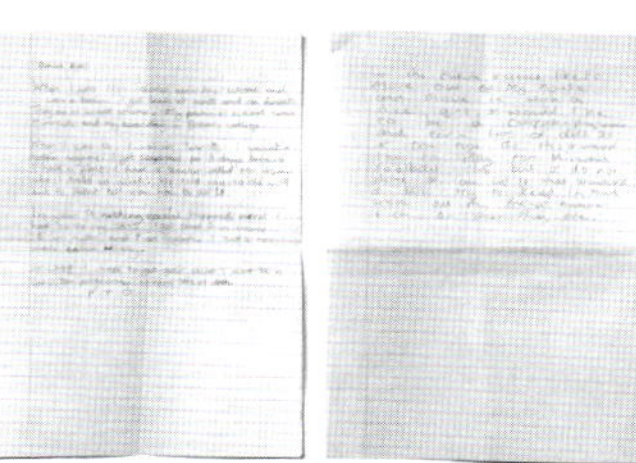

Various photographs with handwritten letters
1994-1996

Including (above) :
Steven, Danny, Daniel, Ryan
black and white print and iris print
above: photograph panel, details from text panel
1996

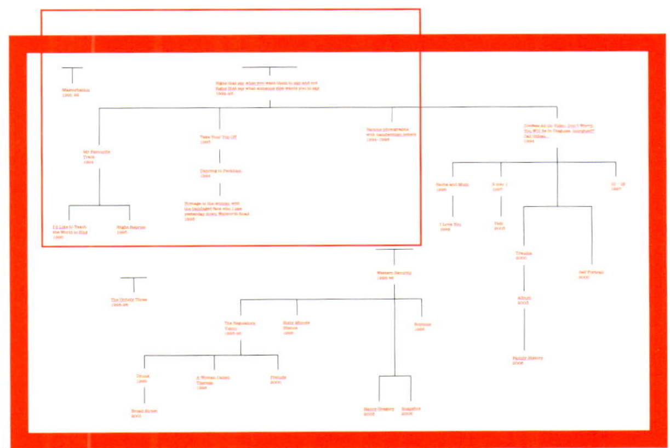

Courtesy Maureen Paley, London

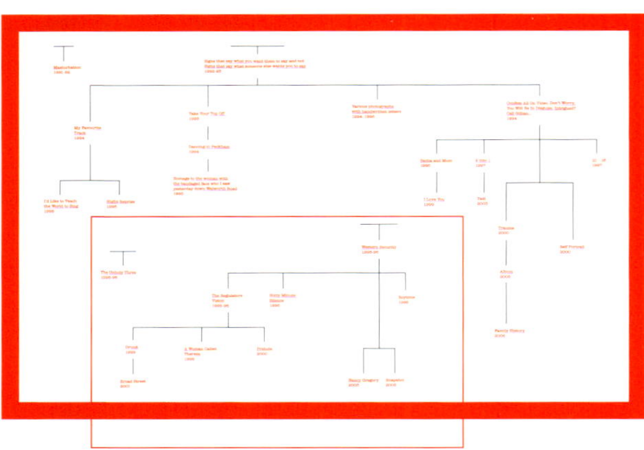

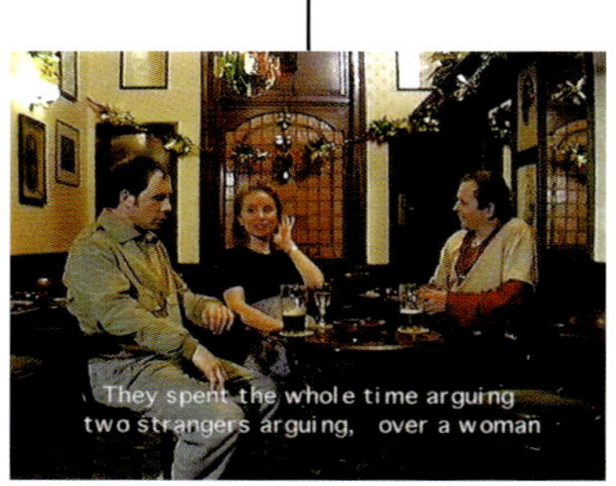

The Unholy Three
3 screen projection with sound
10 minutes
1995-96

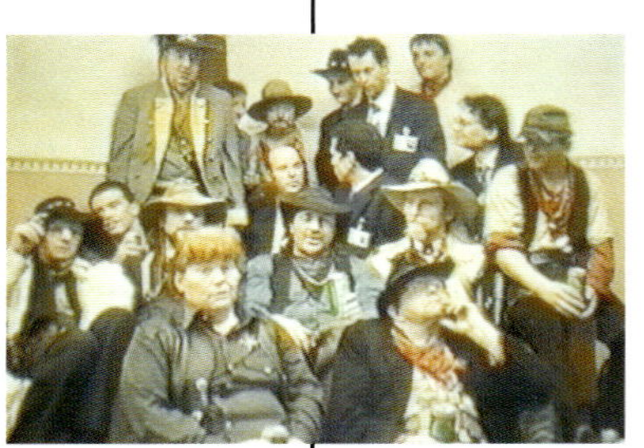

The Regulators Vision
projection with sound
7 minutes
1995-96

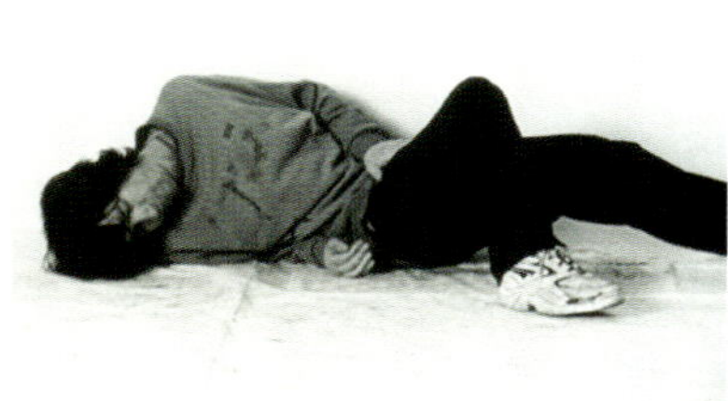

Drunk
3 screen projection
23 minutes
1999

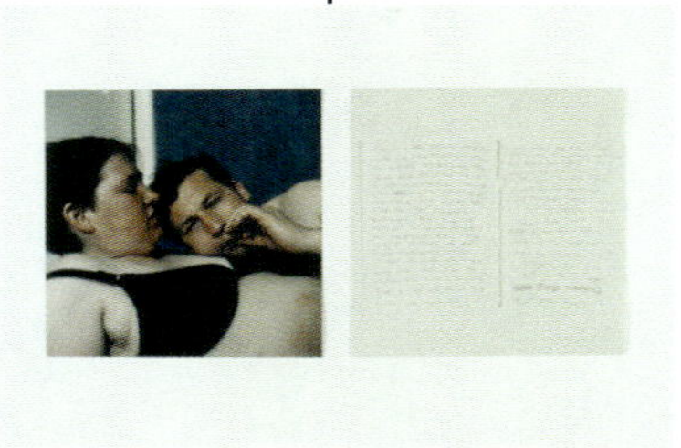

A Woman Called Theresa
Theresa and Mick
c-type prints
1998

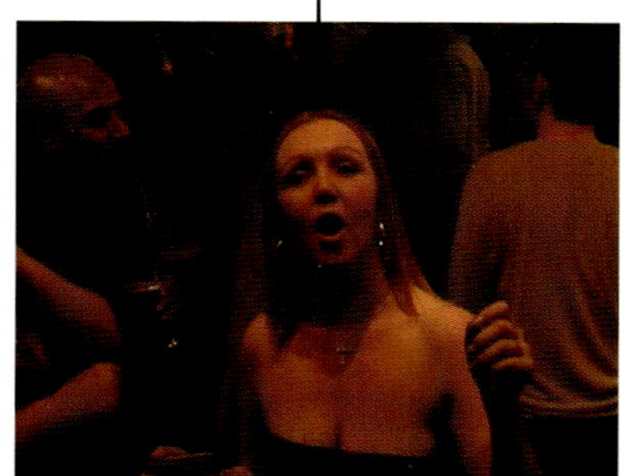

Broad Street
6 screen projection with sound
2001

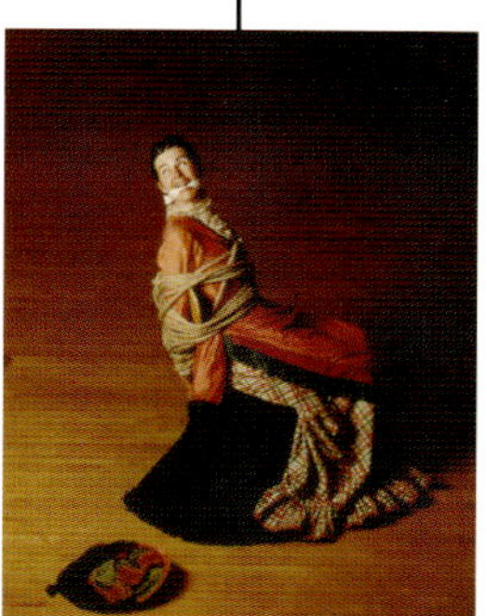

Western Security
10 DVD's for 10 monitors
30 minutes
1995-96

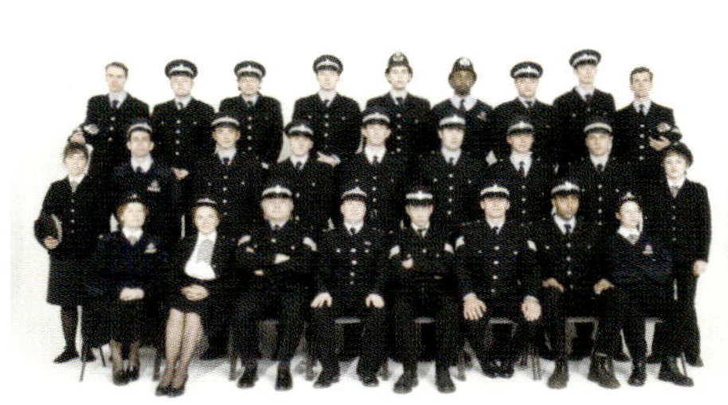

Sixty Minute Silence
projection with sound
60 minutes
1996

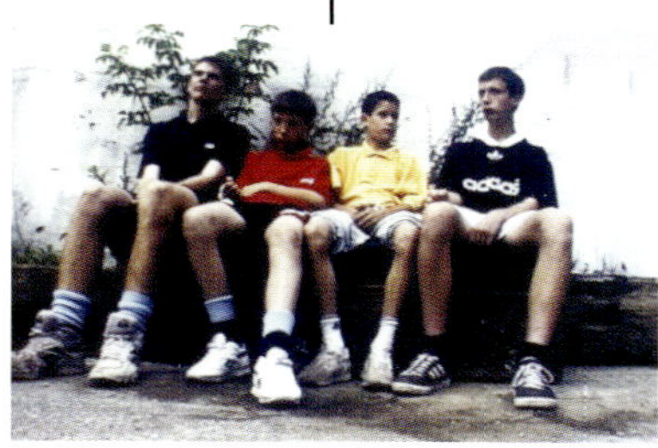

Boytime
projection
1 hour
1996

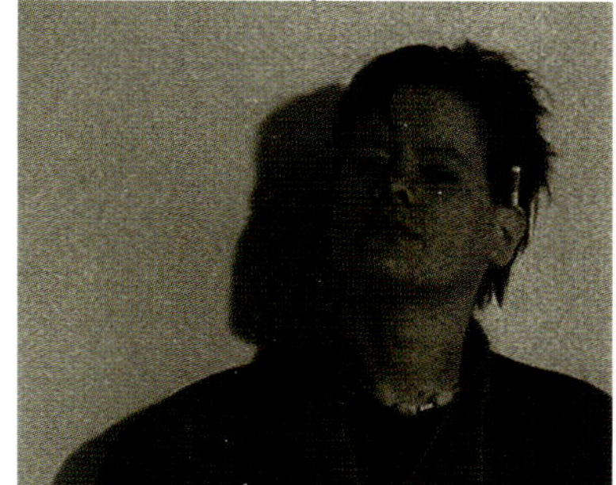

Prelude
projection with sound
2000

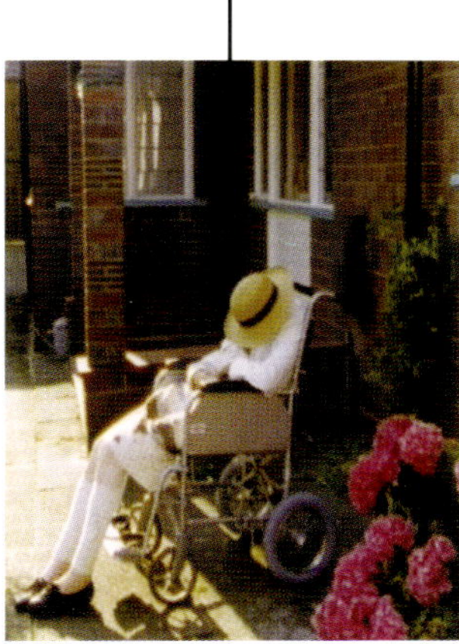

Nancy Gregory
DVD for monitor
and c-type print
2003

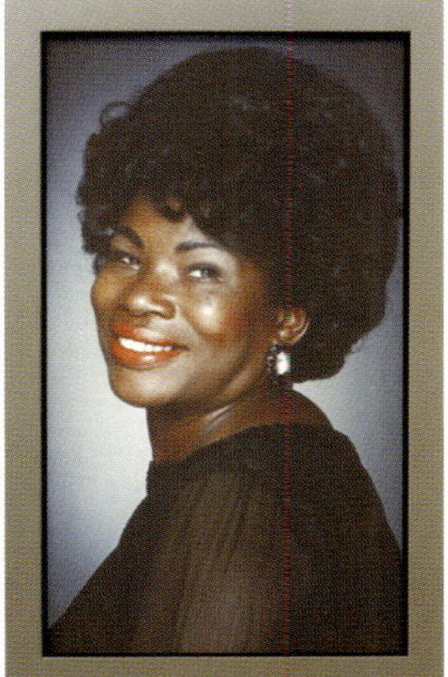

Snapshot
7 DVD's on framed
plasma screens
6 minutes 55 seconds
2005

Courtesy Maureen Paley, London

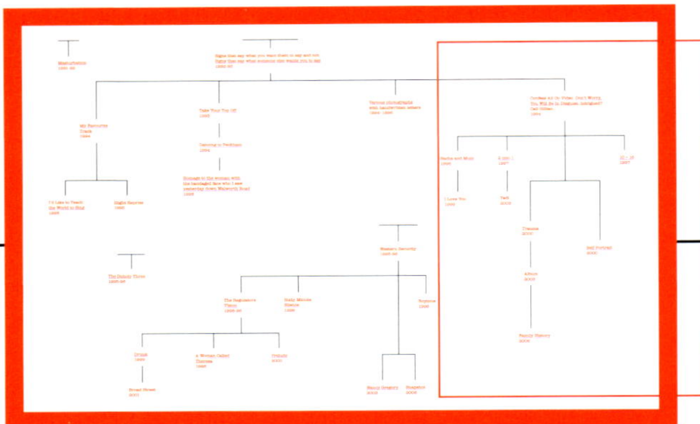

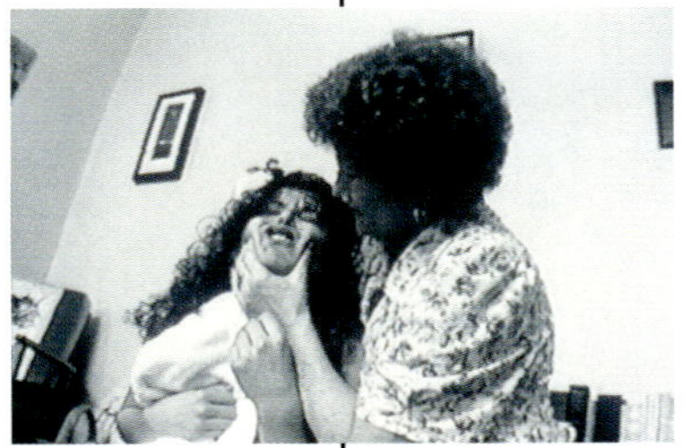

Sacha and Mum
projection with sound
4 minutes 30 seconds
1996

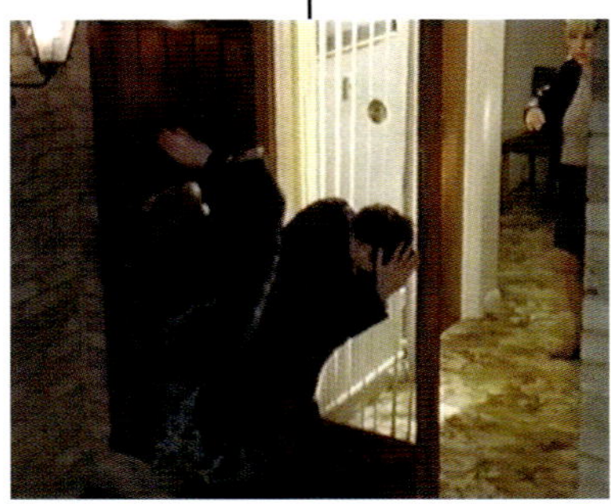

I Love You
projection with sound
1 hour
1999

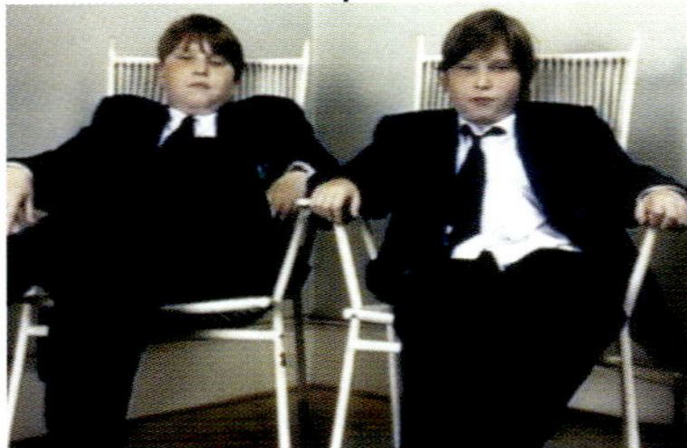

2 into 1
projection with sound
4 minutes 30 seconds
1997

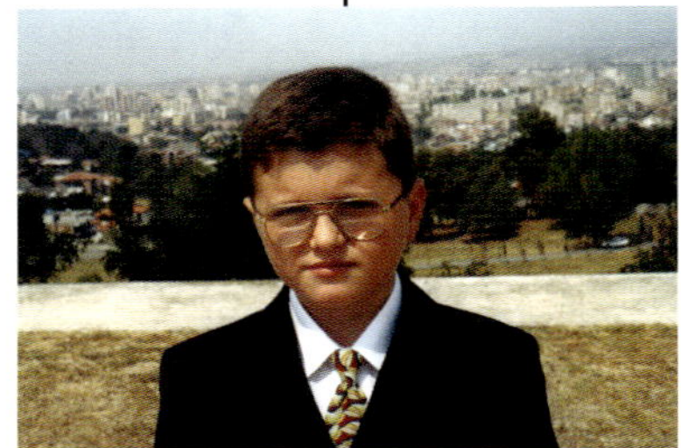

Tedi
projection with sound
3 minutes 46 seconds
2003

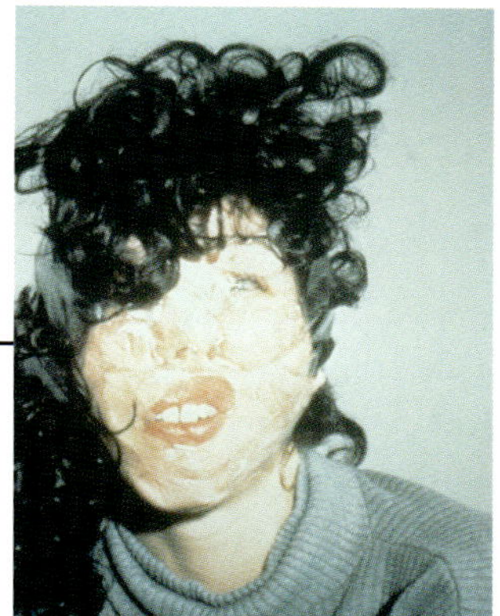

Confess All On Video.
Don't Worry, You Will Be In Disguise.
Intrigued? Call Gillian...
video with sound
30 minutes
1994

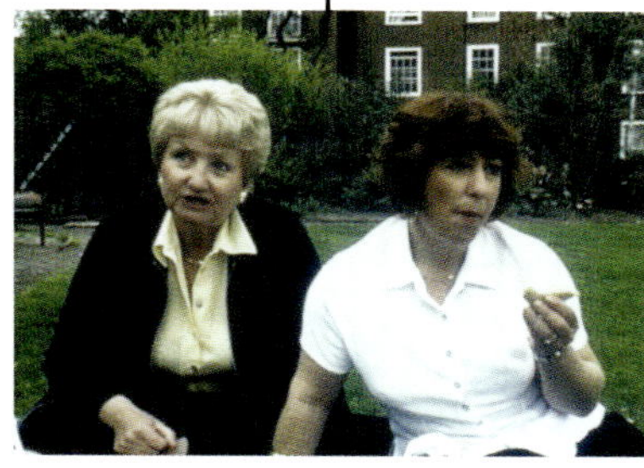

10 – 16
projection with sound
15 minutes
1997

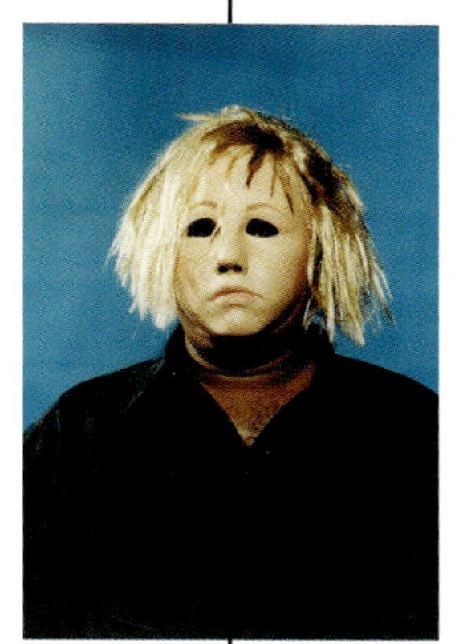

Trauma
back projection
30 minutes
2000

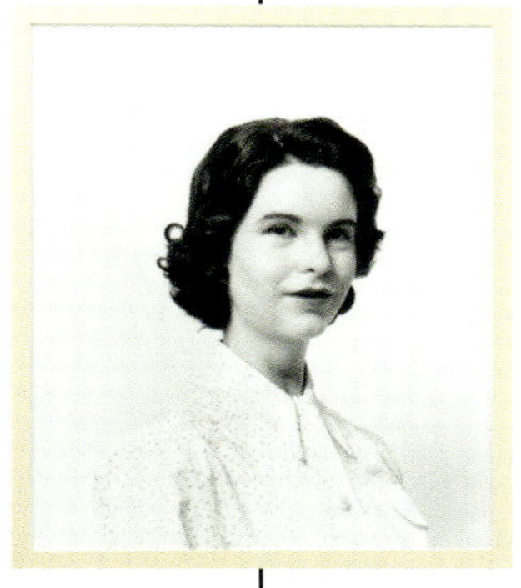

Album

Including (left):
Self Portrait as my
Mother Jean Gregory
black and white print
2003

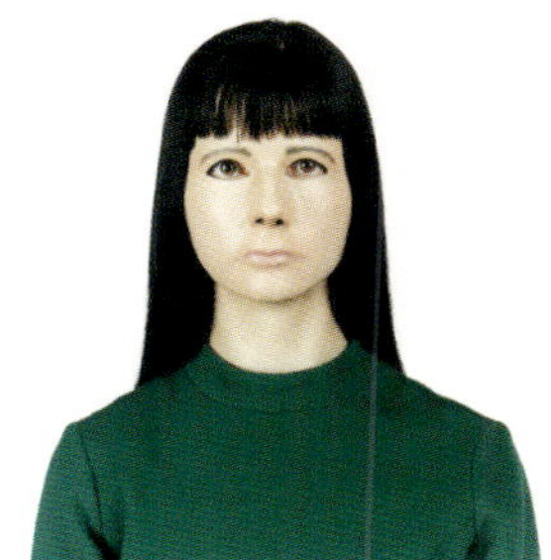

Self Portrait
c-type print
2000

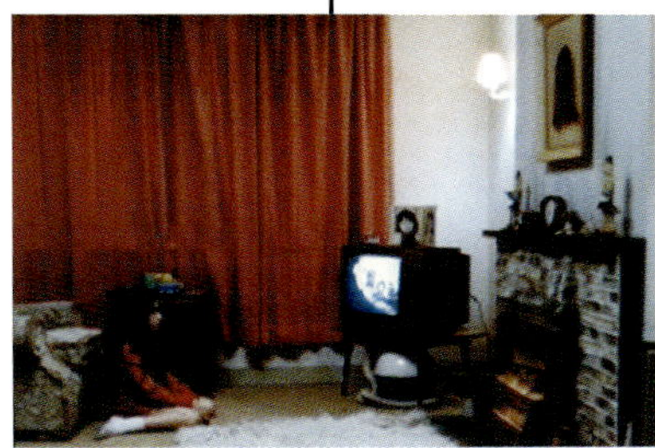

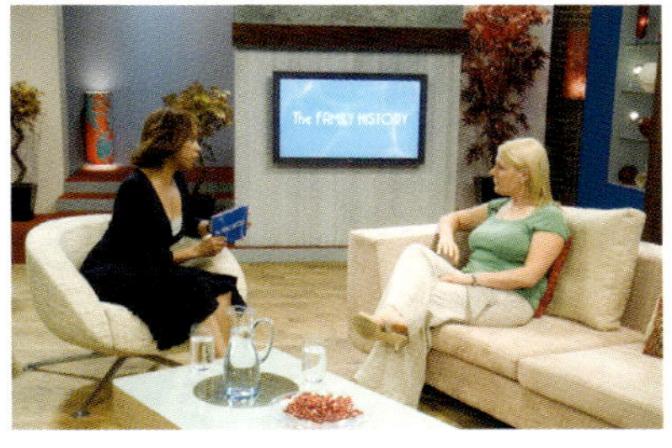

Family History
DVD for projection:
38 minutes 29 seconds
DVD for plasma monitor:
2 minutes 56 seconds
2000

Courtesy Maureen Paley, London

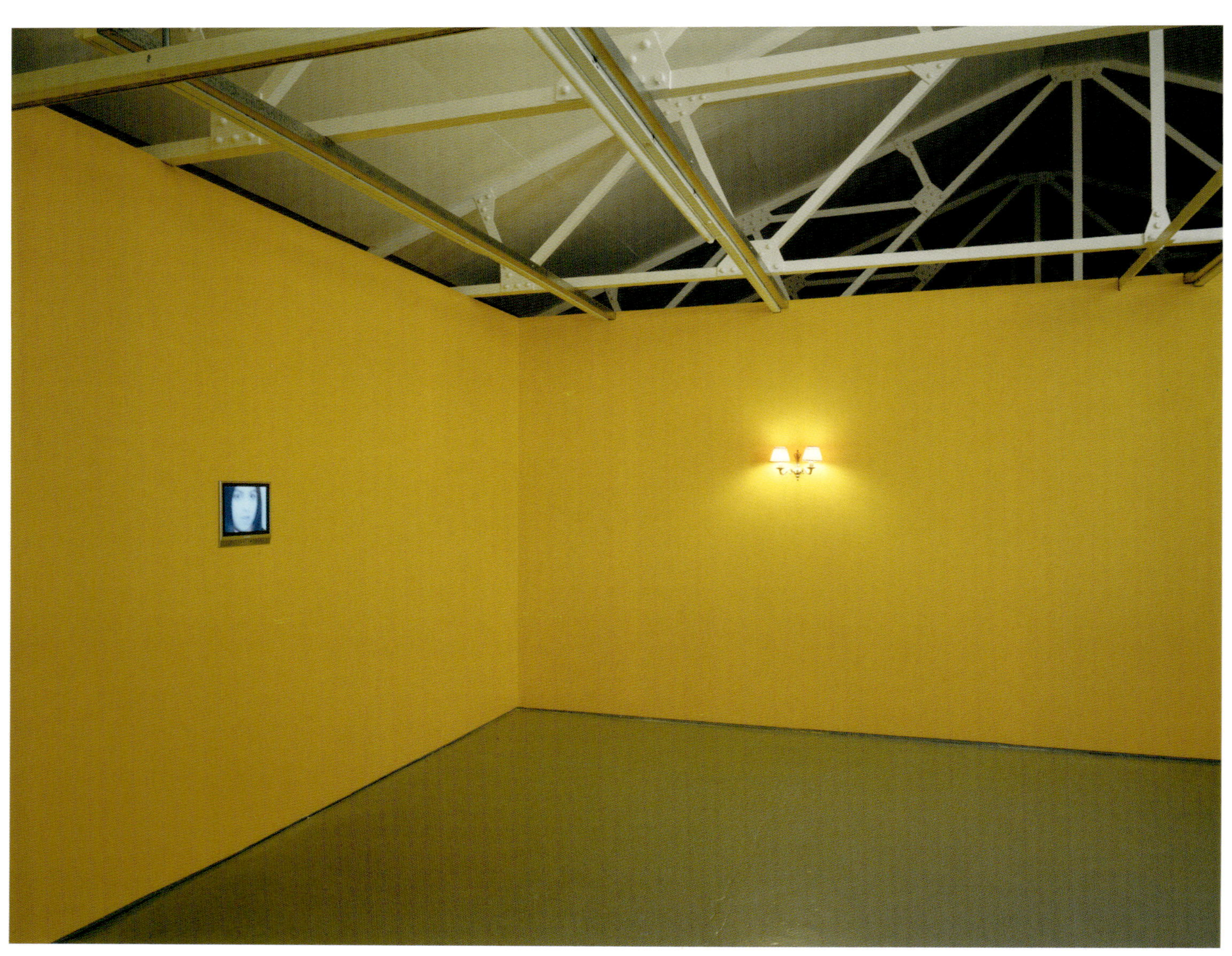

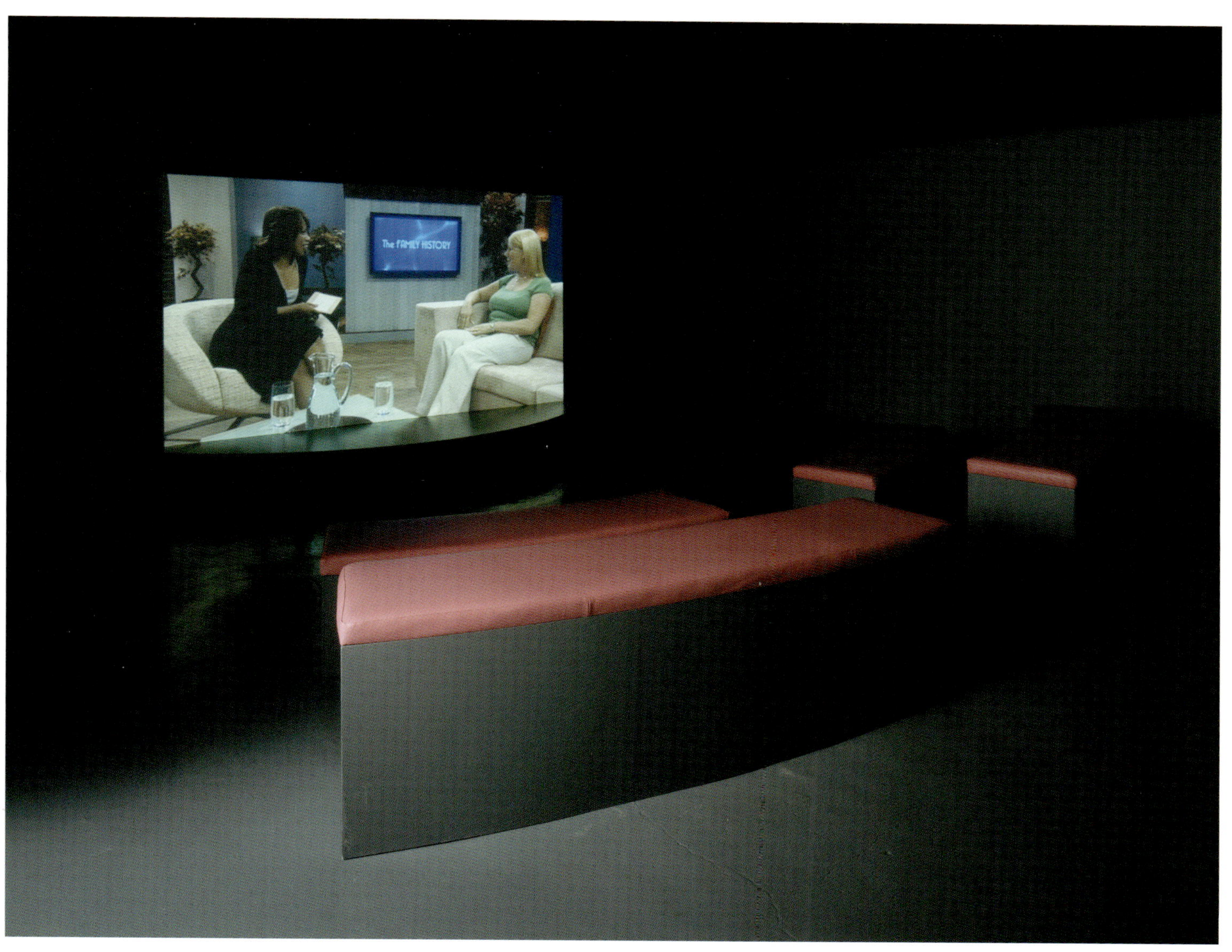

The FAMILY HISTORY

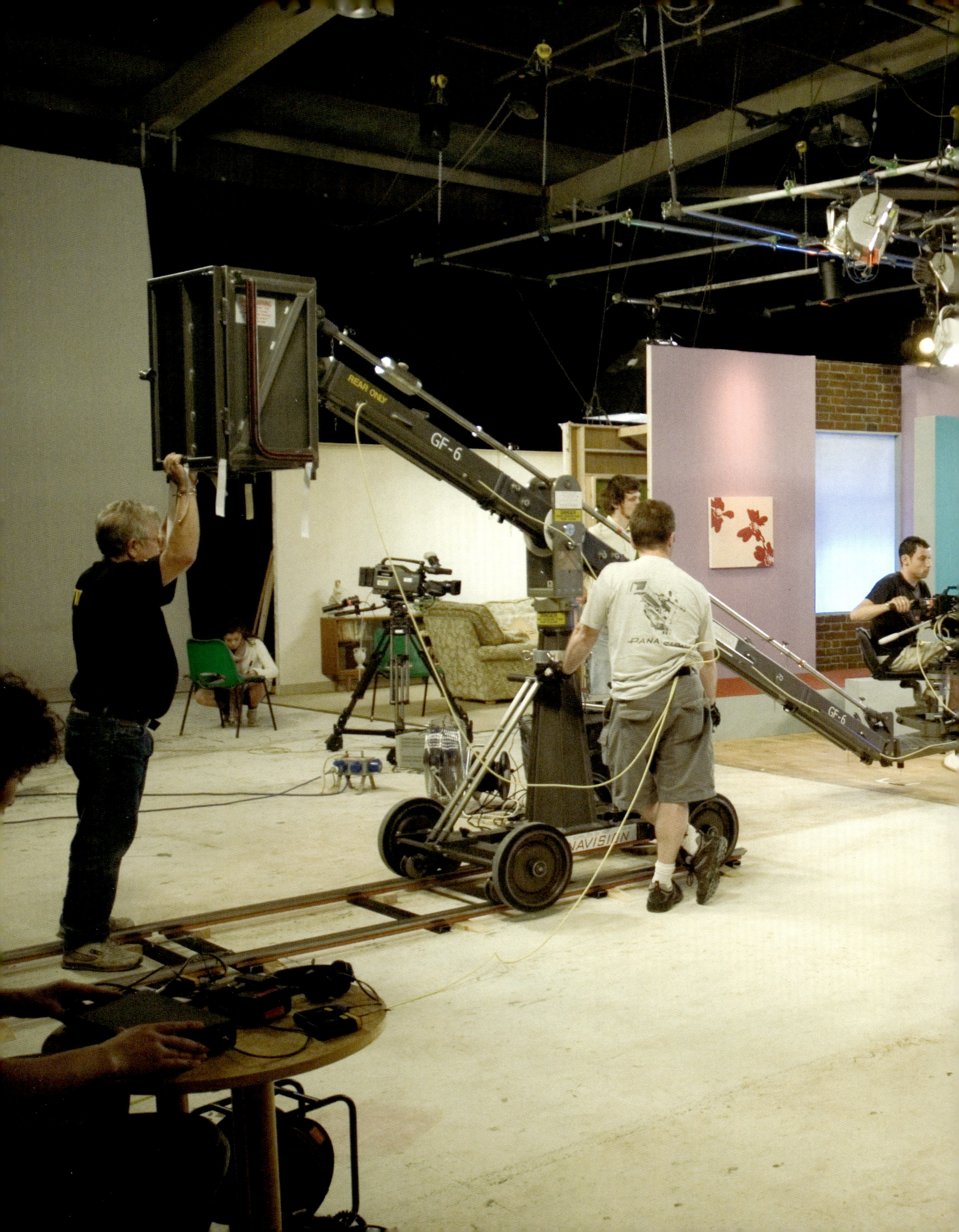

FAMILY HISTORY

'Family History' was commissioned
by Film and Video Umbrella
and Artists in the City, Reading
Borough Council, in association
with Ikon Gallery. Funded by Arts
Council England, with additional
support from Film London Artists'
Moving Image Network. With thanks
to Maureen Paley.

'Family History' was staged at:
The Forbury Hotel Apartments,
Reading, 7 July to 8 August 2006;
Brindley House, Birmingham,
8 September to 10 October 2006;
Maureen Paley, London, 10 October
to 19 November 2006

Reading staging generously
supported by the Waterbridge
Group Ltd and the Forbury Hotel
Apartments. Special thanks to
Tammy Bedford (Reading Borough
Council), and Jim Attewell.

Birmingham staging generously
supported by Midland and City
Developments. Special thanks to
Jan Eldridge, Helen Watkins, Matt
Nightingale, Matt Hogan, Chris
Maggs and Richard Short.

Gillian Wearing would like to thank:
Steven Bode, Bevis Bowden, Nina
Ernst, Caroline Smith and Mike
Jones at Film and Video Umbrella;
Jeni Walwin and Kerry Duggan
at Artists in the City; Jonathan
Watkins and Helen Legg at Ikon
Gallery; Maureen Paley, Dan Gunn,
Max Mugler, Susannah Chisholm
and Oliver Evans at Maureen Paley.

Special thanks to Jean Wearing,
Michael Landy, Helen van der Meij,
Shaun Regen Projects, Chris Knight
and Lisa James.

Artist/Director
GILLIAN WEARING

Cast
MADELINE CASTREY
TRISHA GODDARD
PAIGE SMITH
HEATHER WILKINS

Head of Production
BEVIS BOWDEN

Project Co-ordinator
NINA ERNST

Casting
CHLOE EMMERSON

Production Design
DAVID WEARE

Director of Photography
TEDDY TESTAR

Gaffer
STEVE FINDBERG

Camera Operator 1
JIM DONLEAVY

Camera Operator 2
GARETH HOSKINS

First Camera Assistant
ALEX TAYLOR

Camera Assistant
ROLAND GRAFENSTEIN

Sound Recordist
ROSS ADAMS

Grip
MICKIE PATTEN

Crane Technician
CLIVE TOCHER

Electricians
SAUL HARRIS
MARK STIBBS

Electrician/Desk Operator
NATHAN MATTHEWS

Rigger
MARK SIDE

Hair and Make-up
SARAH EXLEY

Assistant/Researcher
LISA JAMES

Production Assistants
HELEN DOWLING
CLARE TESTAR
RORY HEFFERNAN

Stills Photographer
DAVID PEARSON

Set Construction
PAULO TORRES, SOAP

Fashion Print Design
PHILIP DELAMORE

Costume Maker
LISA ROSE
Digital Fashion Bureau,
London College of Fashion

Post Production
JO McCAFFERY
PEPPER POST PRODUCTION

Editor
FRANKIE PLOWRIGHT

Online Editor
RICHARD CRADICK

Colourist
PETER HARROW

Audio Post Producer
ALEX JENNINGS
SOUND MONSTERS

Dubbing Mixer
SCOTT MARSHALL

Cameras supplied by
BARRY NOAKES
METRO BROADCAST

Location
KATE TUFANO & CLAIRE PEACOCK
GREENFORD STUDIOS

Camera Crane supplied by
PANAVISION

Chaperone
JACQUELINE CASTREY

Catering
LITTLE WOMEN CATERING

Film Processed by TECHNICOLOR

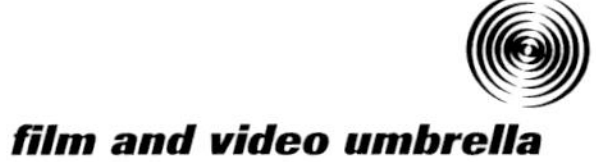

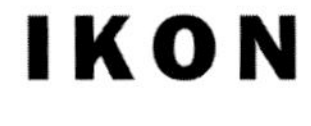

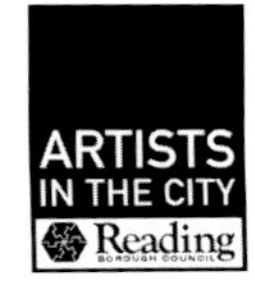

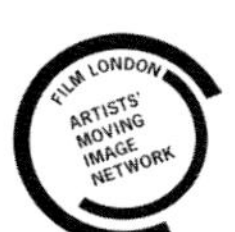

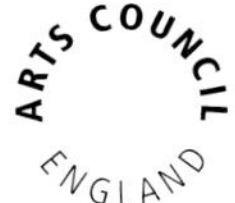